Mark Sarnecki

# The
# Complete Elementary
# Music Rudiments

## 2nd Edition

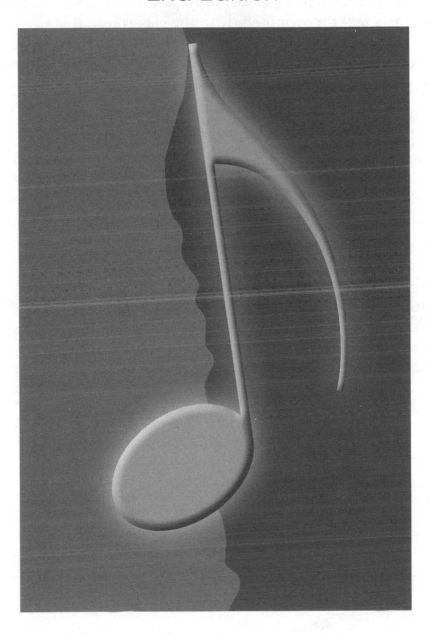

FREDERICK
HARRIS
MUSIC

19 18 17 16 15 14 13   4 5 6 7 8 9 10

# PREFACE

The study of theory is an important part of a complete musical education. Familiarity with the basic concepts of music theory aids in musical literacy, including notation, sight reading, ear training, and memory.

*The Complete Elementary Music Rudiments* is a comprehensive rudiments course covering notation, pitch, the keyboard, rhythm, meter, key signatures, major and minor scales, intervals, chords, modal scales, and beginning harmony.

This book is designed to be used in a number of ways, including self-study, one-on-one music teaching, and as a text for group-study in the classroom. It is suitable for use by all instrumentalists and vocalists. The information is presented in a clear, concise, and systematic manner, and the easy to understand workbook format offers the student plenty of exercises to practice and master the concepts of music rudiments.

Mark Sarnecki

---

*The Complete Elementary Music Rudiments* covers the requirements for the Basic, Intermediate, and Advanced rudiments examinations. The abbreviations for these grades, **B**, **I**, and **A**, appear in the left-hand margin of the page. These symbols indicate the level of the material being covered. The letter **B** refers to Basic Rudiments; the letter **I**, to Intermediate Rudiments; and the letter **A**, to Advanced Rudiments. Basic material is required for the Intermediate level; Basic and Intermediate material is required for the Advanced level.

# CONTENTS

*Music is Sound!*

# MUSIC NOTATION

*notes*
- *pitch*
- *duration*

**S**ound in music is symbolized by **notes**. Notes tell us the pitch (high or low) and the duration (long or short) of sound. Notes are placed on the **staff**, which consists of five lines and four spaces.

Notes are given different names using the first seven letters of the alphabet:

**A B C D E F G**

Signs called **clefs** are placed at the beginning of each staff.

The **treble clef** or G clef curls around the second line of the staff indicating the location of G.

The **bass clef** or F clef has two dots on either side of the fourth line of the staff indicating the location of F.

Here are the names of the notes on the treble and bass staves:

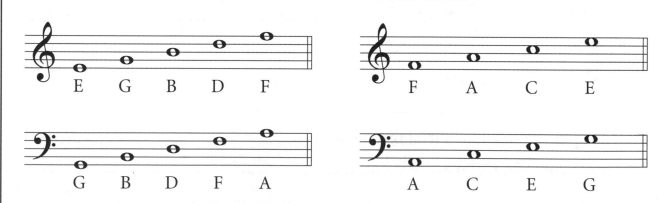

6-11-15

**B**
**I**
**A**

1. Name the following notes.

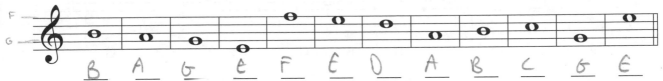

B A G E F E D A B C G E

C G A G D F A B C F G A

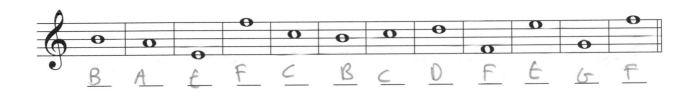

B A E F C B C D F E G F

B D E C G E A G E C F D

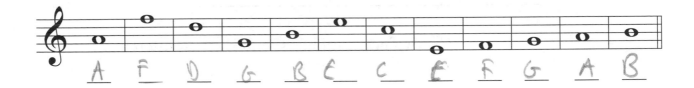

A F D G B E C E F G A B

# MUSIC NOTATION

2. Write the following notes on lines. *whole*

F  G  D  E  B  E  G  D  F  B  G  E

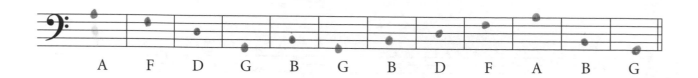

A  F  D  G  B  G  B  D  F  A  B  G

3. Write the following notes in spaces.

F  A  C  E  C  F  A  C  F  E  C  A

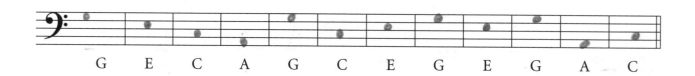

G  E  C  A  G  C  E  G  E  G  A  C

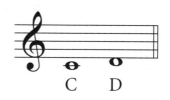

C  D

The two notes, middle C and D, are written just under the treble staff.

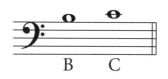

B  C

The two notes, B and middle C, are written just above the bass staff.

Small lines called **ledger lines** are used to extend the range of the staff. These lines are used for notes that are above or below the five lines of the treble and bass staves. The following example includes notes up to three ledger lines above and below the staff, but even more ledger lines may be added above and below if you wish to extend the range of the staff.

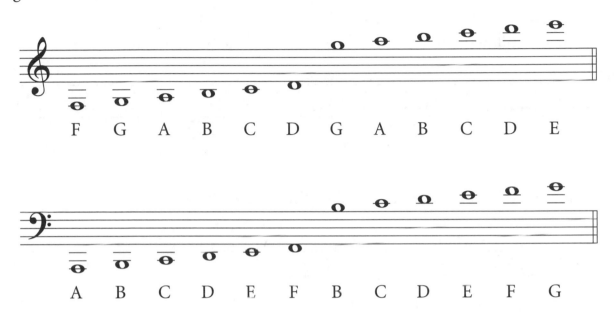

The treble and bass staves combine to make the **grand staff**. The two staves are joined by a straight line and a curved brace or bracket.

*treble + bass staves*

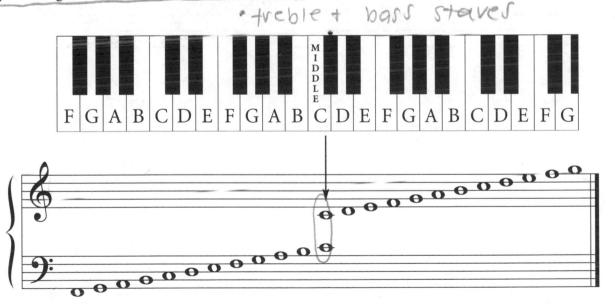

Observe that middle C, a ledger-line note, can be written in both the treble and bass clefs.

# MUSIC NOTATION

**B** **I** **A**

1. Write the following notes using ledger lines above the treble staff.

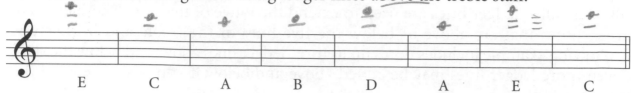

    E       C       A       B       D       A       E       C

2. Write the following notes using ledger lines below the treble staff.

    C       A       F       G       B       A       C       G

3. Write the following notes using ledger lines below the bass staff.

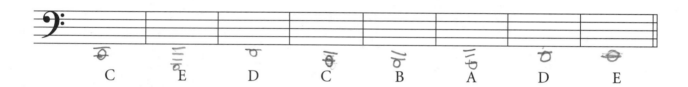

    C       E       D       C       B       A       D       E

4. Write the following notes using ledger lines above the bass staff.

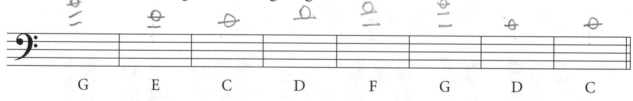

    G       E       C       D       F       G       D       C

5. Write the following notes on the grand staff.

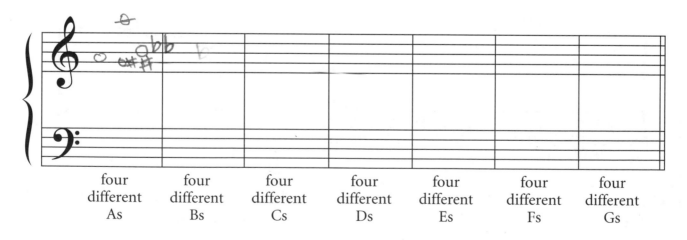

| four different As | four different Bs | four different Cs | four different Ds | four different Es | four different Fs | four different Gs |
|---|---|---|---|---|---|---|

6. Name the following notes.

# C CLEFS

**A**

The example below shows five different C clefs. In past eras, C clefs were in common use, but today only the alto and tenor clefs are used. The groove or opening of these clefs always indicates middle C.

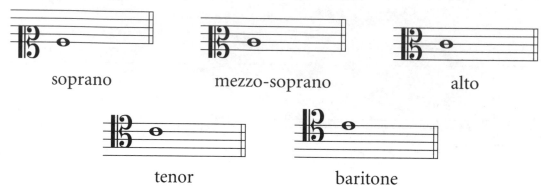

soprano          mezzo-soprano          alto

tenor          baritone

**The Alto Clef**

In the alto clef, middle C is located on the third line of the staff. Music for the viola is written in the alto clef in order to keep most of the notes within the staff. This avoids a large number of ledger lines. The following notes are all middle C.

**A**  1.  Name the following notes.

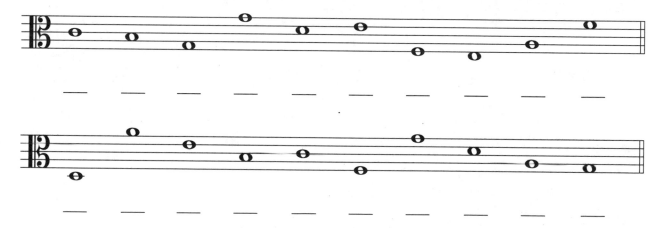

2.  Write the following notes in the alto clef.

D      G      B      F      E      A      C      B      F

3.  Rewrite the following melody, using the alto clef.

Johannes Brahms
(1833–1897)

**A**

### The Tenor Clef

In the tenor clef, middle C is located on the fourth line of the staff. The tenor clef is used for the upper registers of music for bassoon, cello, and trombone. The lower registers for these instruments are written in the bass clef. The following notes are all middle C.

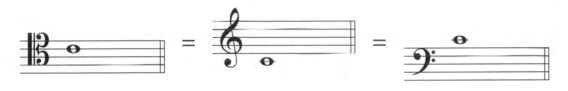

**A**    4.  Write the following notes in the tenor clef.

F    A    B    D    E    G    C    B    F

# MUSIC NOTATION

**A**    5.    Name the following notes.

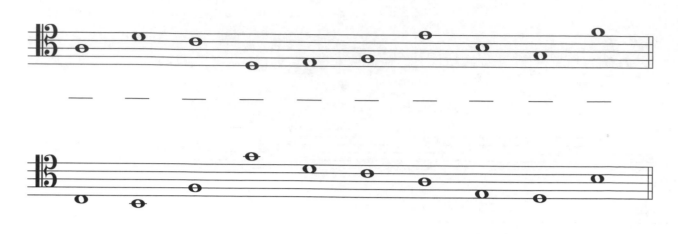

6.    Rewrite the following melody, using the tenor clef.

Johannes Brahms
(1833–1897)

7.    Rewrite the following melody, using the treble clef.

Calixa Lavallée
(1842–1891)

# TIME VALUES

In music, different types of notes are used to indicate different lengths or durations of sound.

Different types of rests are used to indicate different lengths or durations of silence.

| Note | Name | Rest |
|:---:|:---:|:---:|
| 𝅝 | whole note / rest | ▬ |
| 𝅗𝅥 | half note / rest | ▬ |
| ♩ | quarter note / rest | 𝄽 |
| ♪ | eighth note / rest | 𝄾 |
| 𝅘𝅥𝅯 | sixteenth note / rest | 𝄿 |
| 𝅘𝅥𝅰 | thirty-second note / rest | 𝅀 |

When eighth, sixteenth, and thirty-second notes appear alone, they have small curved lines called **flags**. When two or more of these notes occur, they are usually joined by lines called **beams**.

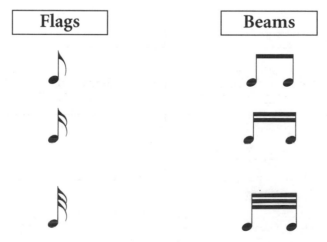

| Flags | Beams |

# RELATIVE NOTE VALUES

**B I A**

| | |
|---|---|
| 1 whole note equals 2 half notes | 𝅝 = 𝅗𝅥 𝅗𝅥 |
| 2 half notes equal 4 quarter notes | 𝅗𝅥 𝅗𝅥 = 𝅘𝅥 𝅘𝅥 𝅘𝅥 𝅘𝅥 |
| 4 quarter notes equal 8 eighth notes | 𝅘𝅥 𝅘𝅥 𝅘𝅥 𝅘𝅥 = 𝅘𝅥𝅮𝅘𝅥𝅮 𝅘𝅥𝅮𝅘𝅥𝅮 𝅘𝅥𝅮𝅘𝅥𝅮 𝅘𝅥𝅮𝅘𝅥𝅮 |
| 8 eighth notes equal 16 sixteenth notes | 𝅘𝅥𝅮𝅘𝅥𝅮 𝅘𝅥𝅮𝅘𝅥𝅮 𝅘𝅥𝅮𝅘𝅥𝅮 𝅘𝅥𝅮𝅘𝅥𝅮 = 𝅘𝅥𝅯𝅘𝅥𝅯𝅘𝅥𝅯𝅘𝅥𝅯 𝅘𝅥𝅯𝅘𝅥𝅯𝅘𝅥𝅯𝅘𝅥𝅯 𝅘𝅥𝅯𝅘𝅥𝅯𝅘𝅥𝅯𝅘𝅥𝅯 𝅘𝅥𝅯𝅘𝅥𝅯𝅘𝅥𝅯𝅘𝅥𝅯 |

| Note | Rest | Name | Number of Beats (in quarter time) |
|---|---|---|---|
| 𝅝 | ▬ | whole | 4 beats |
| 𝅗𝅥 | ▬ | half | 2 beats |
| 𝅘𝅥 | 𝄽 | quarter | 1 beat |
| 𝅘𝅥𝅮 | 𝄾 | eighth | ½ beat |
| 𝅘𝅥𝅯 | 𝄿 | sixteenth | ¼ beat |
| 𝅘𝅥𝅰 | 𝅀 | thirty-second | ⅛ beat |

A dot placed after a note or rest increases the length or duration of that note or rest by half its value.

**In Quarter Time**

| | | |
|---|---|---|
| 𝅝· = 𝅝 + 𝅗𝅥 | **dotted whole** 6 beats | ▬· = ▬ + ▬ |
| 𝅗𝅥· = 𝅗𝅥 𝅘𝅥 | **dotted half** 3 beats | ▬· = ▬ + 𝄽 |
| 𝅘𝅥· = 𝅘𝅥 + 𝅘𝅥𝅮 | **dotted quarter** 1½ beats | 𝄽· = 𝄽 + 𝄾 |
| 𝅘𝅥𝅮· = 𝅘𝅥𝅮 + 𝅘𝅥𝅯 | **dotted eighth** ¾ beats | 𝄾· = 𝄾 + 𝄿 |

1. Write the number of beats that the following notes and rests receive.

𝅘𝅥𝅮 ___1/2___  𝅝 ___4___  𝅗𝅥 ___2___

▬ ___4 or "whole measure"___  𝄽 ___1/2___  𝅘𝅥𝅯 ___1/8___

𝅗𝅥· ___3___  𝅝· ___6___  𝄾 ___1/4___

𝅘𝅥 ___1___  𝅘𝅥𝅮 ___1/4___  𝄾 ___1/2___

𝄿 ___1/8___  ▬ ___2___

Notice where the dots are placed beside notes and rests in the staff. For a note in a space, the dot goes in the same space. For a note on a line, the dot goes in the space above. For a rest, the dot goes in the third space of the staff.

A curved line placed between two notes of the same pitch is called a **tie**. The first note is played and the sound is held for the value of both notes.

There are rules for placing stems on notes. If the note is on the middle line, the stem may go either up or down. Notes above the middle line have stems going down. Notes below the middle line have stems going up.

If a group of notes is to be joined with a beam, the note that is farthest from the third line determines the direction of all the stems under the beam.

If the highest and lowest notes are the same distance from the third line, the position of the stem is determined by where the majority of notes occur. If most notes are above the third line, the stems go down. If most notes are below the third line, the stems go up.

**B**
**I**
**A**

1. Name the type of note.

𝅝  whole     ♩  quarter     ♬  16th

♬  32nd     ♪  eighth     ♩  half

2. Name the type of rest.

𝄿  32nd     𝄼  half     𝄿  eigth

𝄿  16th     𝄽  quarter     𝄻  whole

3. Write one note that is equal to the following groups of notes.

*Standard Practices*

4. Write one rest that is equal to the following notes.

5. Write three notes that are equal to the following dotted notes.

6. Write one note that is equal to the following groups of notes.

7.  Fill in the blanks.

_____4_____ quarter notes equal one whole note.

_____3_____ eighth notes equal one dotted quarter note.

_____8_____ sixteenth notes equal one half note.

×8 _16_____ eighth notes equal one whole note.

_____3_____ half notes equal one dotted whole note.

_____2_____ whole notes equal eight quarter notes.

6_____ sixteenth notes equal one dotted quarter note.

_____4_____ eighth notes equal one half note.

_____3_____ quarter notes equal six eighth notes.

8.  Write one note that is equal to the following tied notes.

9.  Write one rest that is equal to the following groups of rests.

10. Rewrite the following melody, correcting the stem direction as required.

# SEMITONES, WHOLE TONES, AND ACCIDENTALS

*half step*

**B I A**

The piano keyboard is made up of **semitones**. A semitone is the shortest distance between two notes in Western art music. On the keyboard, it is the distance from one key to the next key, black or white. C to C sharp (or D flat) is a semitone. So is E to F.

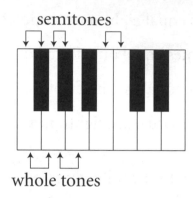

semitones

whole tones

A **whole tone** is made up of two semitones. On the keyboard, a whole tone is any two keys with one key, white or black, between them. Whole tones often have two different letter names in alphabetical order. For example, C to D, F sharp to G sharp, and A flat to B flat are whole tones.

An **accidental** is a sign placed in front of a note that alters its pitch by raising or lowering it.

♯   A **sharp** raises a note by one semitone.

♭   A **flat** lowers a note by one semitone.

♮   A **natural** cancels a sharp or a flat.

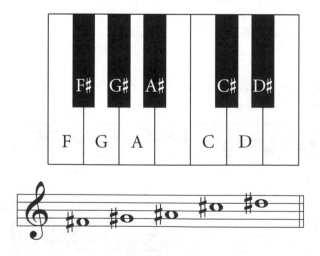

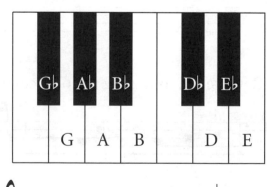

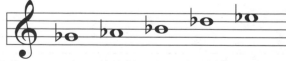

Not all sharps and flats occur on black keys—E sharp, B sharp, F flat, and C flat are played on white keys.

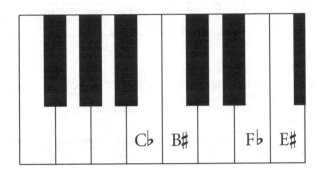

In music, the sharp, flat, or natural signs always go in front of the note, on the same line or space as the note they affect.

However, when you write the letter name of a note, the sharp, flat, or natural sign goes after the note—for example, F♯, B♭.

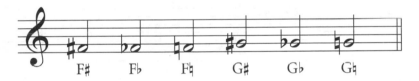

F♯    F♭    F♮    G♯    G♭    G♮

When a note has been altered by an accidental, it remains altered for the remainder of the measure, unless it is changed by a new accidental.

With accidentals, we can change the name of a note without changing its pitch. This type of change is called an **enharmonic** change.

For example, the enharmonic equivalent of F sharp is G flat. The enharmonic equivalent of D sharp is E flat.

1.   Write the following notes on the staves below.

G♭    F♯    E♭    A♭    G♯    D♭    C♯    B♭    G♯    A♯

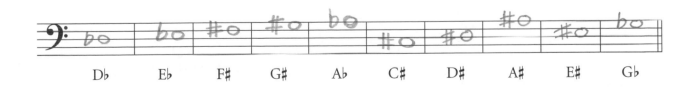

D♭    E♭    F♯    G♯    A♭    C♯    D♯    A♯    E♯    G♭

# SEMITONES, WHOLE TONES, AND ACCIDENTALS

**B I A**

A semitone that consists of two notes with the same letter name is called a **chromatic semitone**.

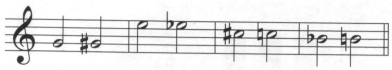

A semitone that consists of two notes with different letter names is called a **diatonic semitone**.

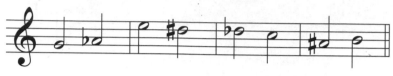

2.  Mark the following as chromatic semitones (CS), diatonic semitones (DS), or whole tones (WT).

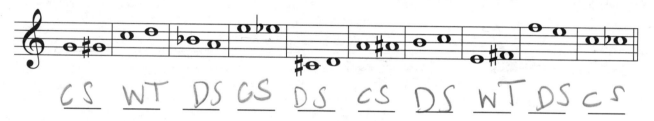

CS   WT   DS   CS   DS   CS   DS   WT   DS   CS

3.  Write chromatic semitones above the following notes.

4.  Write diatonic semitones above the following notes.

*Accidental Rules*

THE COMPLETE ELEMENTARY MUSIC RUDIMENTS

5.  Write diatonic semitones below the following notes.

6.  Write chromatic semitones below the following notes.

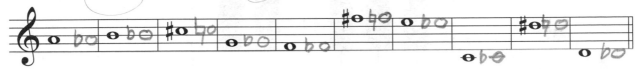

7.  Write whole tones above the following notes.

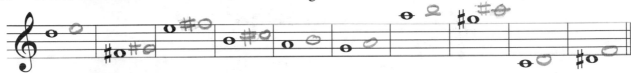

8.  Write whole tones below the following notes.

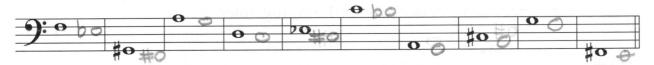

9.  Write the enharmonic equivalents of the following notes.

Ab  G#          G#  Ab          F#  Gb

Bb  A#          C#  Db          Eb  D#

10. Learn the following Italian terms and definitions dealing with tempo.

**B I A**

| Slow | adagio | slow (slower than *andante*, but not as slow as *largo*) |
| | lento | slow |
| | largo | very slow and broad |
| | larghetto | not as slow as *largo* |
| Medium | andante | moderately slow; at a walking pace |
| | andantino | a little faster than *andante* |
| | allegretto | fairly fast (a little slower than *allegro*) |
| | moderato | at a moderate tempo |
| Fast | allegro | fast |
| | presto | very fast |
| | prestissimo | as fast as possible |

# SEMITONES, WHOLE TONES, AND ACCIDENTALS

✗ The **double sharp** sign raises a natural note one whole tone (two semitones), or raises a note that is sharp one semitone without changing its letter name.

♭♭ The **double flat** lowers a natural note one whole tone (two semitones), or lowers a flattened note one semitone without changing its letter name.

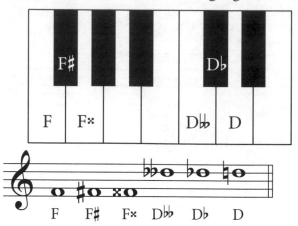

Every note, with the exception of G sharp/A flat, can have three names.

1. Write chromatic semitones above the following notes.

2. Write diatonic semitones above the following notes.

3. Write whole tones above the following notes.

4. Write chromatic semitones below the following notes.

5. Write diatonic semitones below the following notes.

6. Write whole tones below the following notes.

# MAJOR SCALES

B I A

A **scale** is a series of notes in succession. There are several types of scales. Each scale has a specific combination of tones and semitones.

The **major scale** is the most common scale. It is built using the following pattern of tones and semitones:

**tone – tone – semitone – tone – tone – tone – semitone**

If we build a scale starting on C following this pattern of tones and semitones, we get the C major scale. Every scale degree can be numbered. The note that the scale is built upon, no matter where it is placed in the octave, is always referred to as scale degree $\hat{1}$. A caret sign ( ^ ) placed above a number identifies that number as a scale degree.

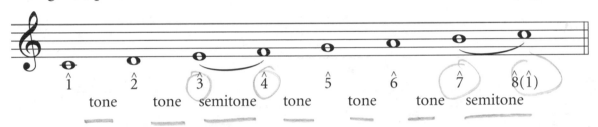

In a major scale, there are semitones between notes $\hat{3}$ and $\hat{4}$, and notes $\hat{7}$ and $\hat{8}(\hat{1})$. Whole tones occur between the other notes. In the above example, the semitones are indicated with a short, curved line called a **slur**.

By following this pattern, we can build major scales starting on any note. If we begin the scale on G, we must use an accidental (in this case, F sharp) to produce the pattern of tones and semitones that makes this scale major.

If we follow this pattern of tones and semitones beginning on the note F, we get a scale with one flat (B flat).

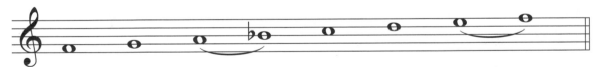

The first note of the major scale is called the **tonic.** The scale has the same name as its tonic. For example, the major scale that begins with D is called the D major scale; the major scale that begins with B flat is called the B flat major scale.

When a piece of music is based on a particular scale, it is said to be in that **key**. A piece based on the C major scale is in the key of C major. A piece based on the F major scale is in the key of F major.

## MAJOR SCALES

1. Add accidentals to make major scales. Name each scale. Mark the semitones with a slur.

scale name: _____ D major _____

scale name: _____ A major _____

scale name: _____ E major _____

scale name: _____ Bb major _____

scale name: _____ Eb major _____

scale name: _____ Ab major _____

*THE COMPLETE ELEMENTARY MUSIC RUDIMENTS*

When a piece of music is based on a specific scale, it contains the accidentals that are found in that scale. Instead of writing the accidentals in front of every note, composers collect all the accidentals at the beginning of each staff immediately after the clef. This is called a **key signature.** This indicates all the sharps or flats that must be played.

Here is the scale of D major using accidentals:

Here is the scale of D major using a key signature:

Sharps and flats are grouped in a specific order when placed on the staff.

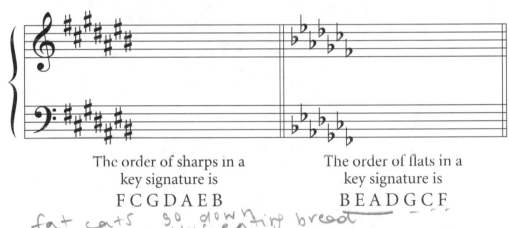

The order of sharps in a
key signature is
F C G D A E B

The order of flats in a
key signature is
B E A D G C F

*fat cats go down allys eating breot*

Every note or degree of a scale has a specific name. This is the list of the names for the degrees of the scale:

$\hat{1}$   **Tonic** — *Root - Scale*
$\hat{2}$   **Supertonic**
$\hat{3}$   **Mediant**
$\hat{4}$   **Subdominant**
$\hat{5}$   **Dominant**
$\hat{6}$   **Submediant** — *also relative minor*
$\hat{7}$   **Leading note**
$\hat{8}$   **Tonic ($\hat{1}$)**

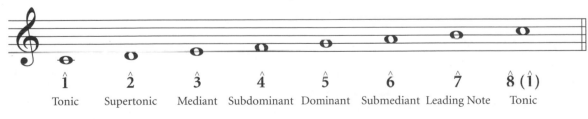

| $\hat{1}$ | $\hat{2}$ | $\hat{3}$ | $\hat{4}$ | $\hat{5}$ | $\hat{6}$ | $\hat{7}$ | $\hat{8}$ ($\hat{1}$) |
|---|---|---|---|---|---|---|---|
| Tonic | Supertonic | Mediant | Subdominant | Dominant | Submediant | Leading Note | Tonic |

## B I A — THE CIRCLE OF FIFTHS

The **circle of fifths** relates keys by 5ths. We start with a circle divided into twelve sections, like a clock, with C in the "12" position.

The sharp keys are set to the right (moving clockwise) in order of the number of sharps in their key signatures.

The flat keys are set to the left (moving counterclockwise) in order of the number of flats in their key signatures.

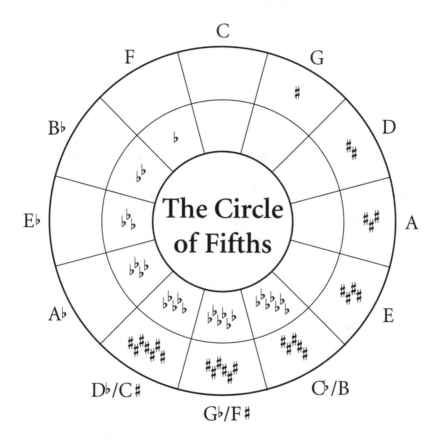

This arrangement of keys shows two things:

1.    The distance between each key and the next is a 5th.

2.    Three pairs of keys share the same spots in the circle:

        D flat/C sharp, G flat/F sharp and C flat/B.

These three pairs of keys are **enharmonic**—they have the same pitch but the notes are named differently.

**B**
**I**
**A**

1.   Write the following key signatures on the grand staff.

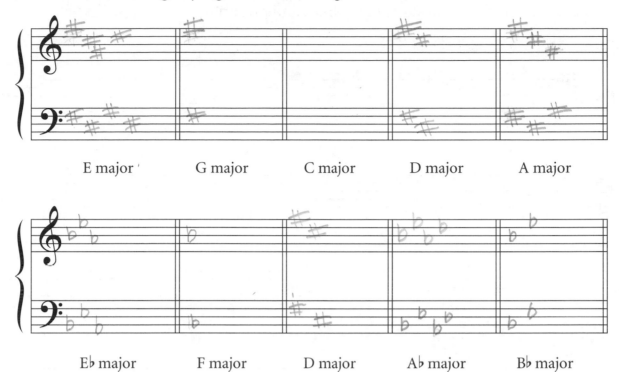

| E major | G major | C major | D major | A major |

| E♭ major | F major | D major | A♭ major | B♭ major |

2.   Identify the following key signatures.

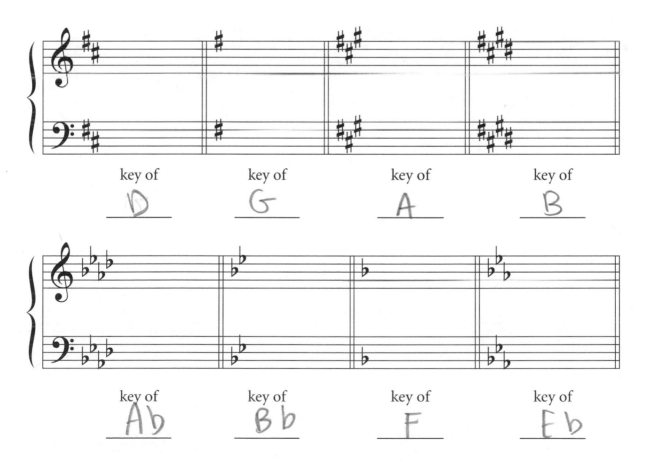

| key of | key of | key of | key of |
| D | G | A | B |

| key of | key of | key of | key of |
| A♭ | B♭ | F | E♭ |

## MAJOR SCALES

B
I
A

3. Write the following scales, ascending and descending, using key signatures. Label the tonic (T), subdominant (SD), and dominant (D) notes.

A major

D major

G major

E major

F major

E♭ major

A♭ major

B♭ major

C major

4. For the following notes, name the major key and the degree of the scale: tonic (T), subdominant (SD), or dominant (D).

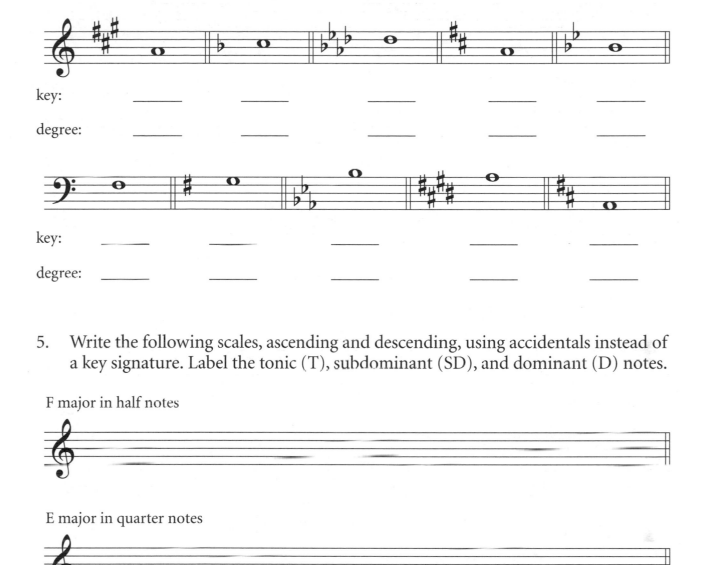

key: _____  _____  _____  _____  _____

degree: _____  _____  _____  _____  _____

key: _____  _____  _____  _____  _____

degree: _____  _____  _____  _____  _____

5. Write the following scales, ascending and descending, using accidentals instead of a key signature. Label the tonic (T), subdominant (SD), and dominant (D) notes.

F major in half notes

E major in quarter notes

A♭ major in single eighth notes

D major in dotted half notes

# MAJOR SCALES

Eb major in single sixteenth notes

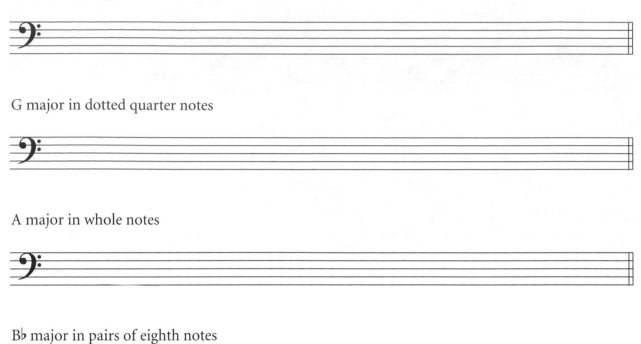

G major in dotted quarter notes

A major in whole notes

Bb major in pairs of eighth notes

6.  Write the following key signatures.

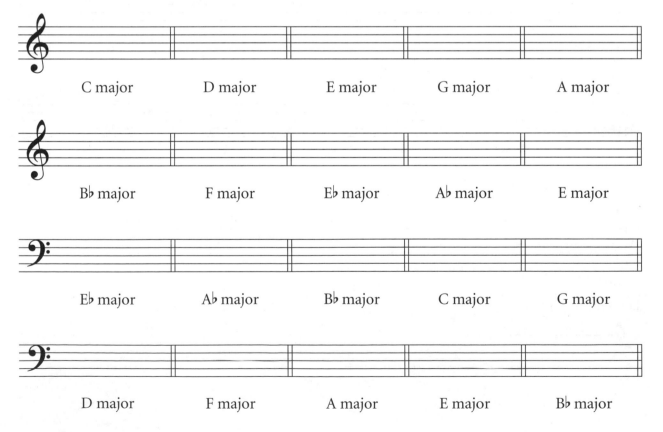

| C major | D major | E major | G major | A major |

| Bb major | F major | Eb major | Ab major | E major |

| Eb major | Ab major | Bb major | C major | G major |

| D major | F major | A major | E major | Bb major |

7. Write the following notes using key signatures.

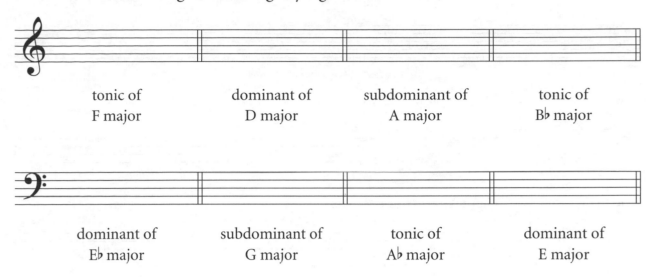

tonic of
F major

dominant of
D major

subdominant of
A major

tonic of
B♭ major

dominant of
E♭ major

subdominant of
G major

tonic of
A♭ major

dominant of
E major

8. Write the following scales, ascending and descending, using key signatures.

The major scale with a key signature of three flats

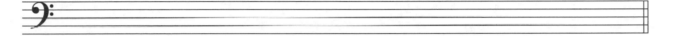

The major scale with G as the dominant

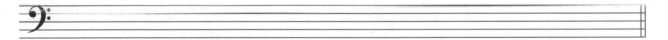

The major scale with a key signature of two sharps

The major scale with D as the subdominant

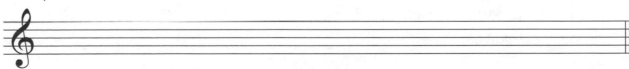

The major scale with B as the dominant

## MAJOR SCALES

The major scale with a key signature of one sharp

The major scale with A♭ as the tonic

The major scale with a key signature of two flats

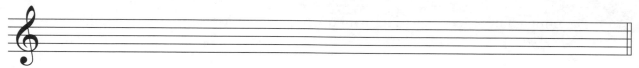

The major scale with B♭ as the subdominant

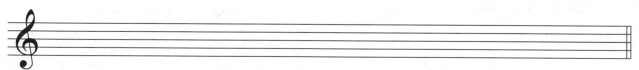

9.  Learn the following Italian terms and their definitions.

| | |
|---|---|
| *cantabile* | in a singing style |
| *con pedale, con ped.* | with pedal |
| *D.C. al Fine* | repeat from the beginning and end at *Fine* |
| *dolce* | sweet |
| *fine* | the end |
| *grazioso* | graceful |
| *legato* | smooth |
| *maestoso* | majestic pace |
| *mano destra, M.D.* | right hand |
| *mano sinistra, M.S.* | left hand |
| *marcato* | marked or stressed |
| *tenuto* | held, sustained |

**I**
**A**
1.  Write the following notes, using key signatures on the grand staves below.

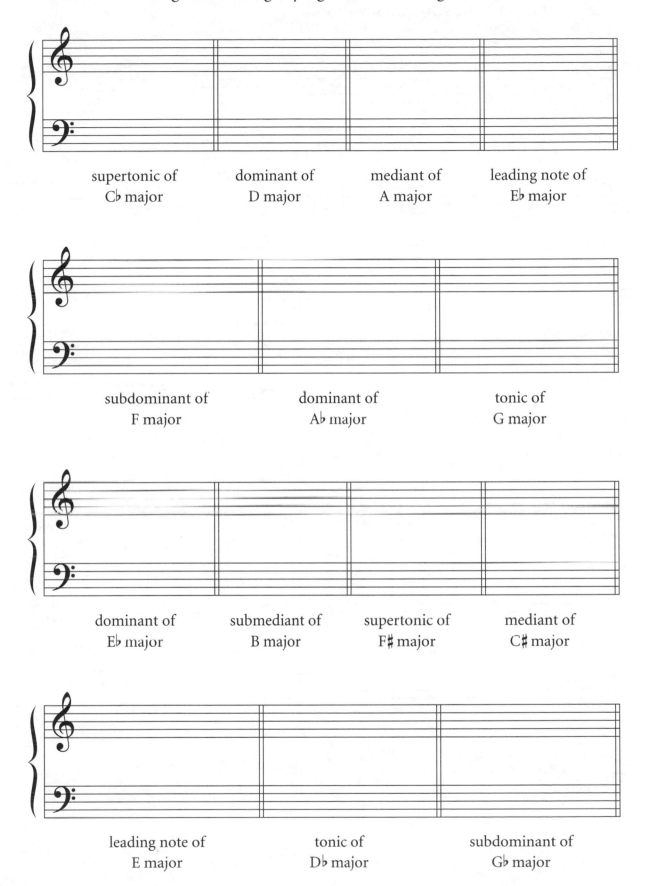

supertonic of
C♭ major

dominant of
D major

mediant of
A major

leading note of
E♭ major

subdominant of
F major

dominant of
A♭ major

tonic of
G major

dominant of
E♭ major

submediant of
B major

supertonic of
F♯ major

mediant of
C♯ major

leading note of
E major

tonic of
D♭ major

subdominant of
G♭ major

## MAJOR SCALES

2. Write the following scales in half notes, ascending and descending, using key signatures. Mark the semitones with a slur.

B major

C♭ major

F♯ major

A♭ major

E major

G♭ major

D♭ major

C♯ major

3. Write the following scales, ascending and descending, in whole notes, using key signatures.

The major scale with C♯ as the dominant

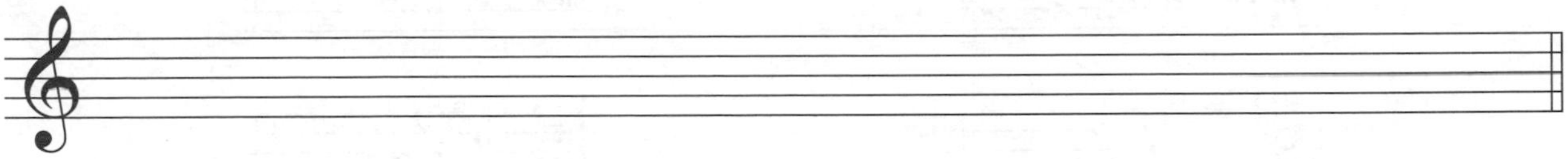

The major scale with six flats in the key signature

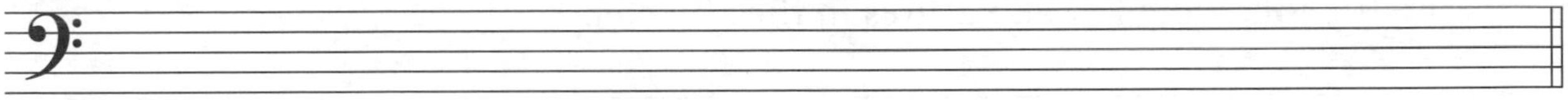

The major scale with B♭ as the leading note

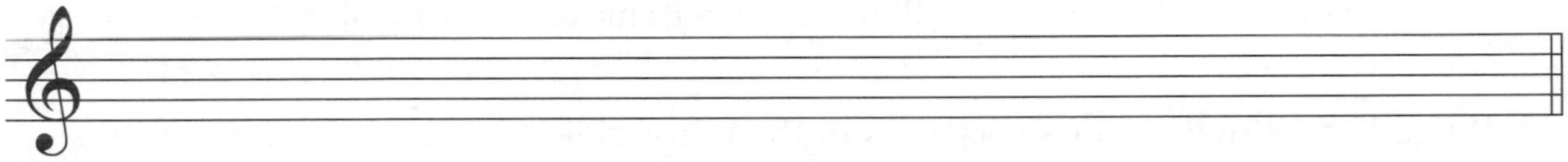

The major scale with two sharps in the key signature

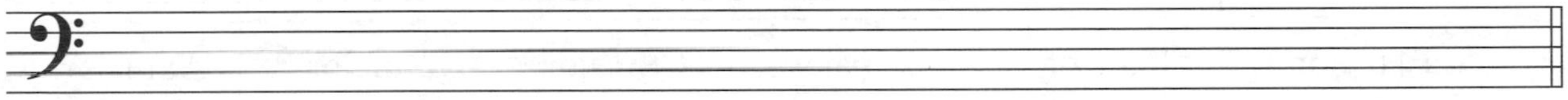

The major scale with F as the supertonic

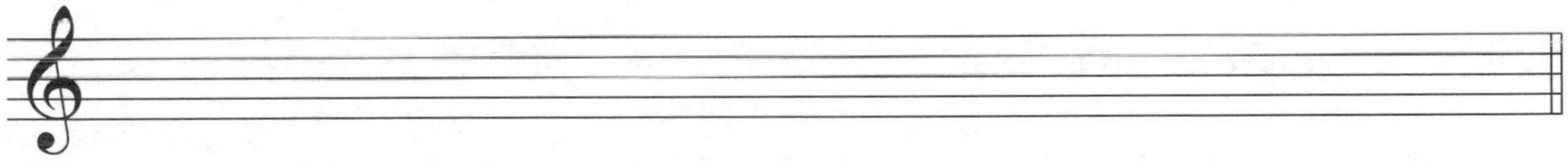

The major scale with three sharps in the key signature

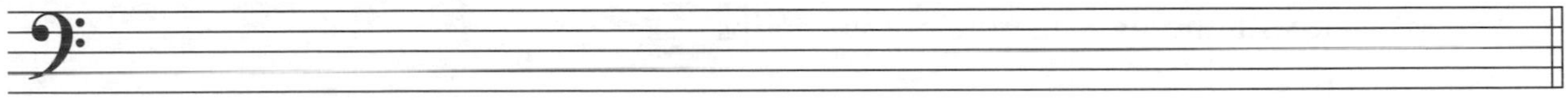

The major scale with F as the mediant

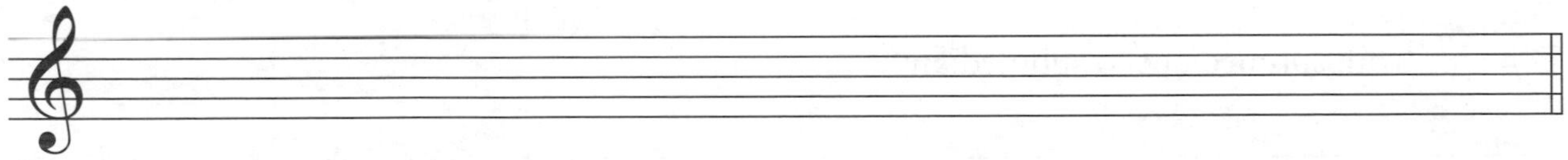

The major scale with D♭ as the subdominant

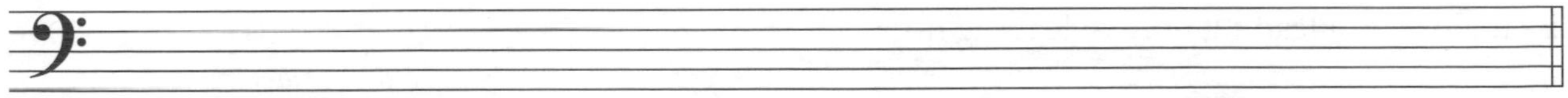

## MAJOR SCALES

**A**

Here is the placement of key signatures on the alto and tenor staves.

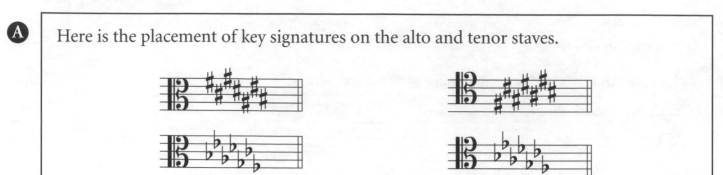

1. Write the following key signatures in the alto clef.

    A major      Gb major      B major      Bb major      C# major      Ab major

2. Write the following key signatures in the tenor clef.

    F# major      E major      Gb major      C# major      Bb major      Ab major

3. Write the following scales in the tenor clef using key signatures.

C# major from supertonic to supertonic

The major scale with the key signature of four sharps

D major from submediant to submediant

Eb major from leading note to leading note

4. Write the following scales in the alto clef, ascending and descending, using key signatures.

Cb major

F# major from dominant to dominant

The major scale with a key signature of one flat

Gb major from submediant to submediant

A major from subdominant to subdominant

The major scale with a key signature of three sharps

G major

E major from mediant to mediant

# MINOR SCALES

For each major key, there is a **relative minor key**. Major and minor keys that are related use the same key signature. The relative minor of a major key is three semitones *lower*.

For example, the relative minor of C major is A minor. They have the same key signature: no sharps or flats.

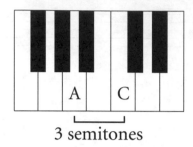

3 semitones

## RELATIVE MAJOR AND MINOR KEYS

| Major Keys | Sharps and Flats | Minor Keys |
|---|---|---|
| C | — | A |
| G | F♯ | E |
| D | F♯, C♯ | B |
| A | F♯, C♯, G♯ | F♯ |
| E | F♯, C♯, G♯, D♯ | C♯ |
| B | F♯, C♯, G♯, D♯, A♯ | G♯ |
| F♯ | F♯, C♯, G♯, D♯, A♯, E♯ | D♯ |
| C♯ | F♯, C♯, G♯, D♯, A♯, E♯, B♯ | A♯ |
| F | B♭ | D |
| B♭ | B♭, E♭ | G |
| E♭ | B♭, E♭, A♭ | C |
| A♭ | B♭, E♭, A♭, D♭ | F |
| D♭ | B♭, E♭, A♭, D♭, G♭ | B♭ |
| G♭ | B♭, E♭, A♭, D♭, G♭, C♭ | E♭ |
| C♭ | B♭, E♭, A♭, D♭, G♭, C♭, F♭ | A♭ |

To find the relative major of a minor key, count *up* three semitones. For example, the relative major of B minor is D major.

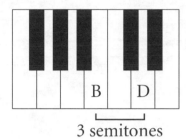

3 semitones

A major scale and a minor scale that have the same tonic are called **tonic major** and **tonic minor.** For example, F major is the tonic major of F minor and F minor is the tonic minor of F major.

1.  Name the relative minor of the following major keys.

   D major _____     F major _____     G major _____

   A major _____     E major _____     B♭ major _____

   E♭ major _____     A♭ major _____     C major _____

2.  Name the major and minor keys for the following key signatures.

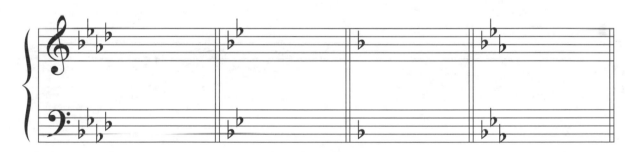

major key:     _____        _____        _____        _____

minor key:     _____        _____        _____        _____

# MAJOR SCALES

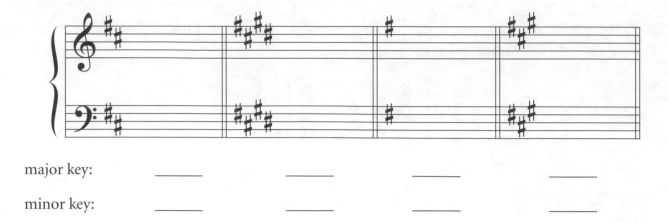

major key: _____  _____  _____  _____

minor key: _____  _____  _____  _____

**B**
**I**
**A**

When a minor scale is written with no accidentals, it is called a **natural minor scale**.

The E natural minor scale has the same key signature (F sharp) as G major, its relative major. In a natural minor scale, there are semitones between notes $\hat{2}$ and $\hat{3}$ and notes $\hat{5}$ and $\hat{6}$.

1.  Write the following natural minor scales using key signatures. Mark the semitones.

E minor in quarter notes

B minor in half notes

D minor in whole notes

G minor in eighth notes

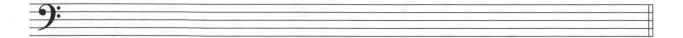

C# minor in dotted half notes

C minor in dotted quarter notes

F# minor in sixteenth notes

The **harmonic minor scale** is formed by raising the seventh degree of the natural minor scale. Notice that *the raised leading note is not in the key signature.*

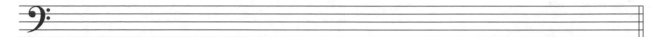

The E harmonic minor scale has the same key signature (F sharp) as G major, its relative major, but the seventh degree of the scale (D sharp) is raised with an accidental.

In a harmonic minor scale, there are semitones between notes $\hat{2}$ and $\hat{3}$, $\hat{5}$ and $\hat{6}$, and $\hat{7}$ and $\hat{8}$.

The scale of C harmonic minor has a key signature of three flats (B flat, E flat, and A flat). The natural on the seventh degree of the scale raises the B flat one semitone to B natural.

# MINOR SCALES

1. Complete the following harmonic minor scales by adding the correct key signature and raising the seventh degree of the scale. Name each scale. Mark the semitones.

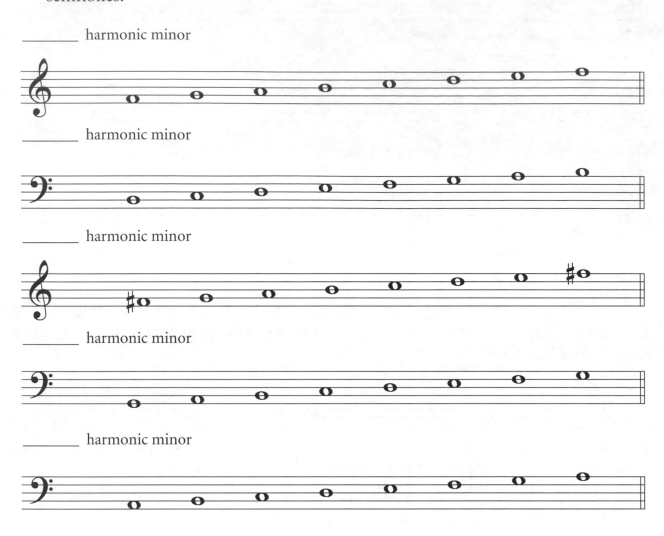

_____ harmonic minor

_____ harmonic minor

_____ harmonic minor

_____ harmonic minor

_____ harmonic minor

2. Write the following scales, ascending and descending, using key signatures. Label the tonic (T), subdominant (SD), and dominant (D) notes.

F harmonic minor

G harmonic minor

C# harmonic minor

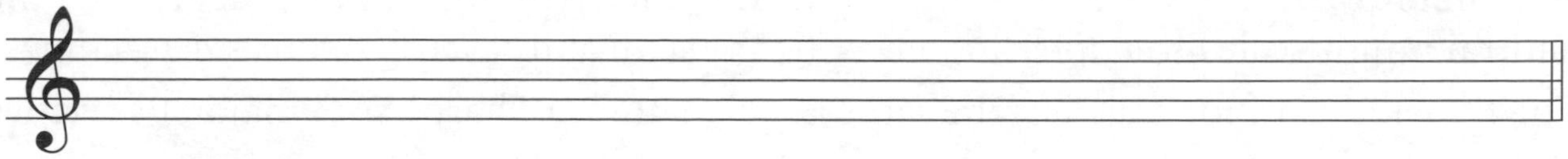

B harmonic minor

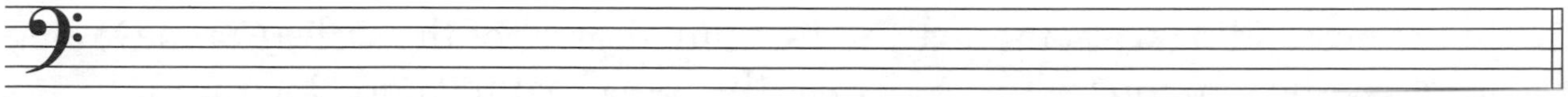

F# harmonic minor

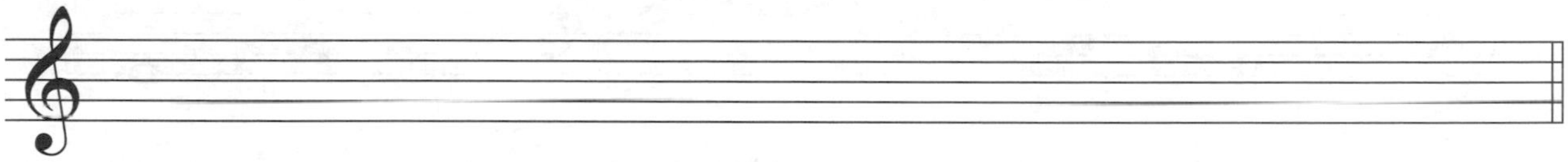

E harmonic minor

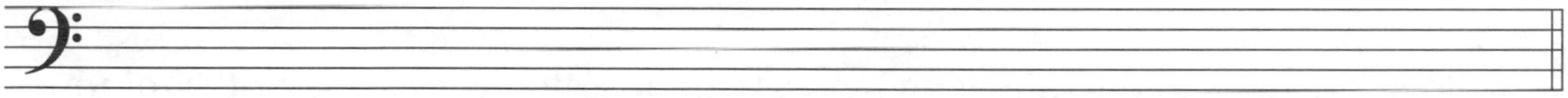

C harmonic minor

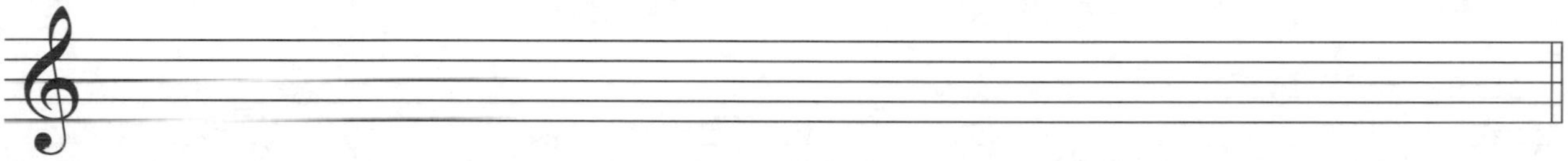

D harmonic minor

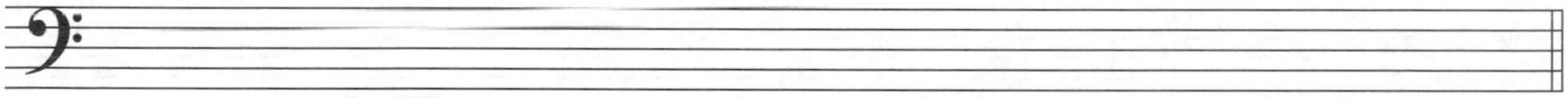

## MINOR SCALES

The **melodic minor scale** is formed by *raising* the sixth and seventh degrees of the natural minor scale *ascending,* and *lowering* the sixth and seventh degrees *descending.*

The E melodic minor scale has the same key signature (F sharp) as G major, its relative major, but

(1)  in the ascending scale, the sixth and seventh degrees of the scale (C and D) are raised one semitone (to C sharp and D sharp).

(2)  in the descending scale, the sixth and seventh degrees of the scale (C and D) are lowered one semitone with accidentals (back to C natural and D natural).

In a melodic minor scale, semitones occur between notes $\hat{2}$ and $\hat{3}$ and notes $\hat{7}$ and $\hat{8}$ ascending, and between notes $\hat{2}$ and $\hat{3}$ and notes $\hat{5}$ and $\hat{6}$ descending.

1.  Add accidentals to the following natural minor scales to create melodic minor scales. Name each scale. Mark the semitones.

_____ melodic minor

_____ melodic minor

_____ melodic minor

_____ melodic minor

_____ melodic minor

_____ melodic minor

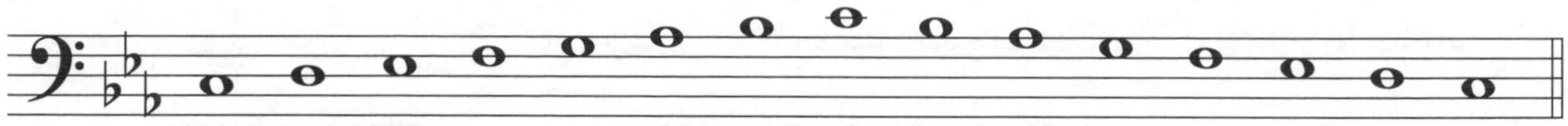

_____ melodic minor

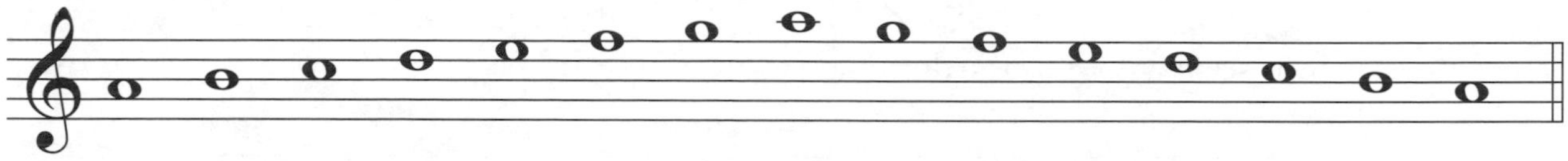

2.   Write the following scales, ascending and descending, using key signatures. Label the tonic (T), subdominant (SD), and dominant (D) notes.

F♯ melodic minor

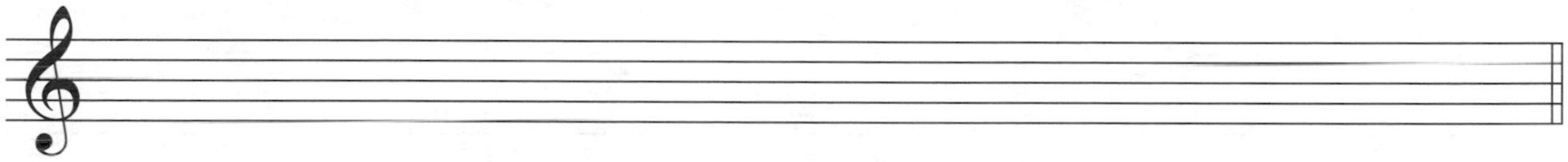

D melodic minor

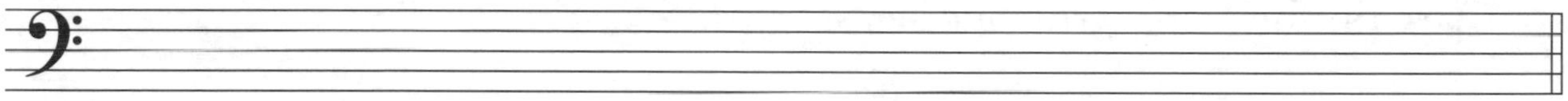

A melodic minor

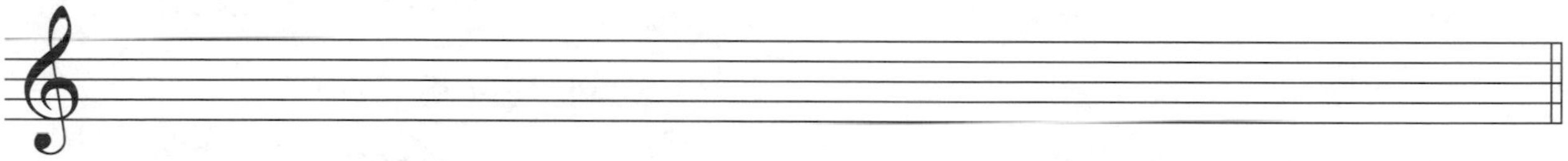

C melodic minor

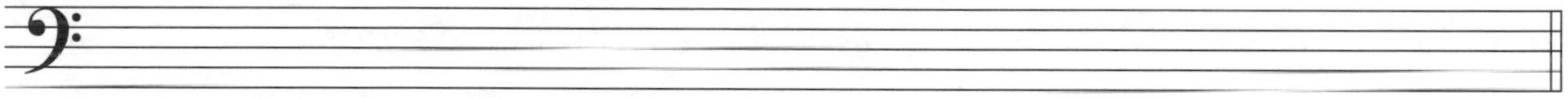

B melodic minor

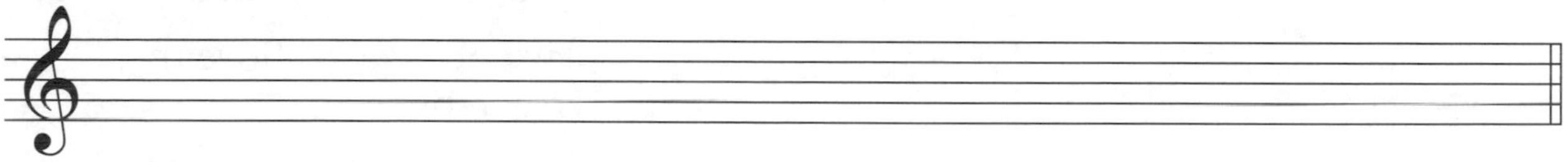

F melodic minor

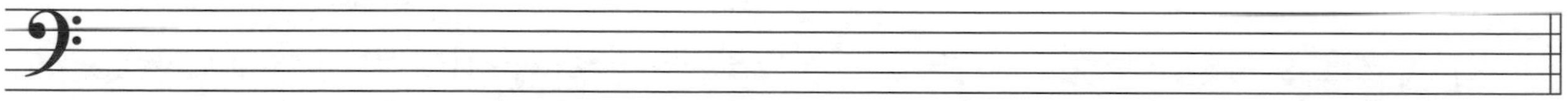

E melodic minor

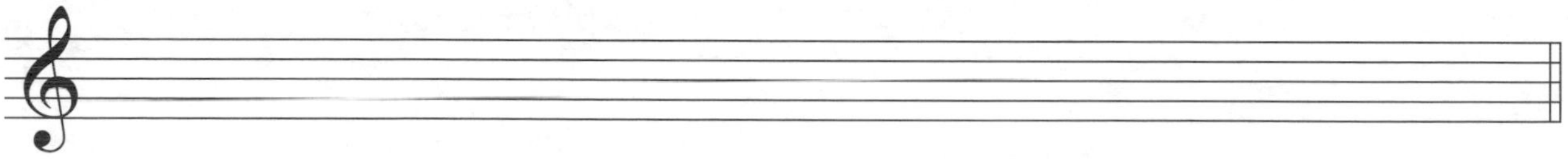

C♯ melodic minor

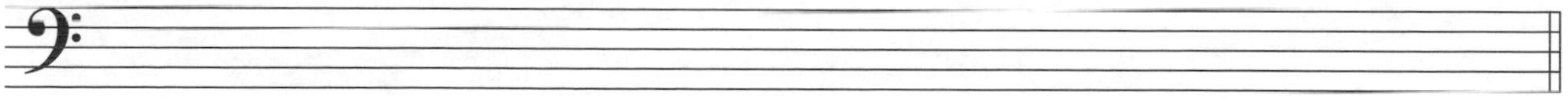

## Minor Scales

3.  Write the following scales, ascending and descending, using key signatures.

The harmonic minor scale with a key signature of three flats

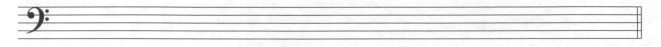

The natural minor scale with A as the dominant

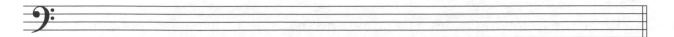

The melodic minor scale with a key signature of one sharp

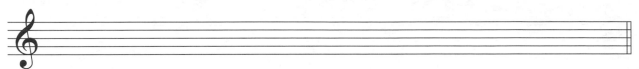

4.  Learn the following terms and signs.

**B**
**I**
**A**

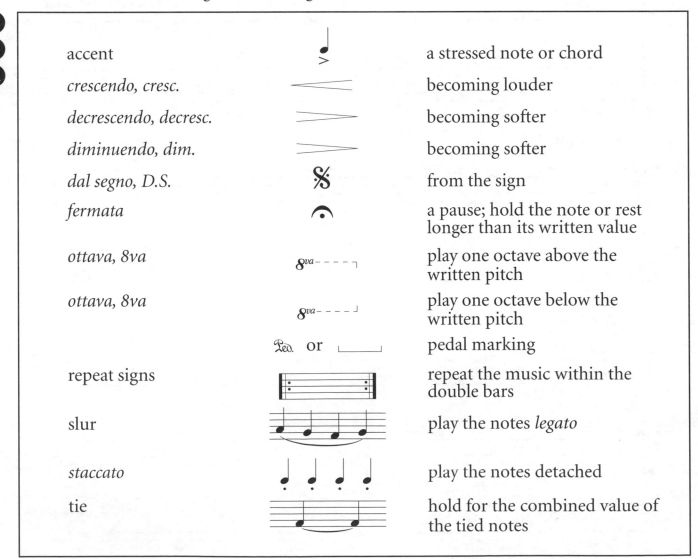

| | | |
|---|---|---|
| accent | | a stressed note or chord |
| *crescendo, cresc.* | | becoming louder |
| *decrescendo, decresc.* | | becoming softer |
| *diminuendo, dim.* | | becoming softer |
| *dal segno, D.S.* | | from the sign |
| *fermata* | | a pause; hold the note or rest longer than its written value |
| *ottava, 8va* | 8va- - - - | play one octave above the written pitch |
| *ottava, 8va* | 8va- - - - | play one octave below the written pitch |
| | Ped. or | pedal marking |
| repeat signs | | repeat the music within the double bars |
| slur | | play the notes *legato* |
| *staccato* | | play the notes detached |
| tie | | hold for the combined value of the tied notes |

5. Add clefs, key signatures, and any necessary accidentals to create the following scales.

A harmonic minor

B melodic minor

F natural minor

D harmonic minor

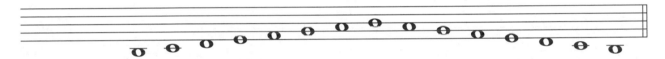

C melodic minor

E natural minor

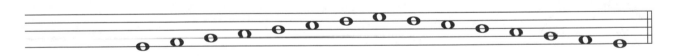

B harmonic minor

## MINOR SCALES

1. Fill in the blanks.

| Major Key | Key Signature | Relative Minor Key |
|-----------|---------------|--------------------|
| C♯ major | _____ | _____ |
| G♭ major | _____ | _____ |
| F♯ major | _____ | _____ |
| B major | _____ | _____ |
| D♭ major | _____ | _____ |
| C♭ major | _____ | _____ |

2. Name the key and type of minor scale (natural, harmonic, melodic) for the examples below.

scale of _____

scale of _____

scale of _____

scale of _____

scale of _____

3. Write the following scales, ascending and descending, using key signatures.

D harmonic minor in half notes

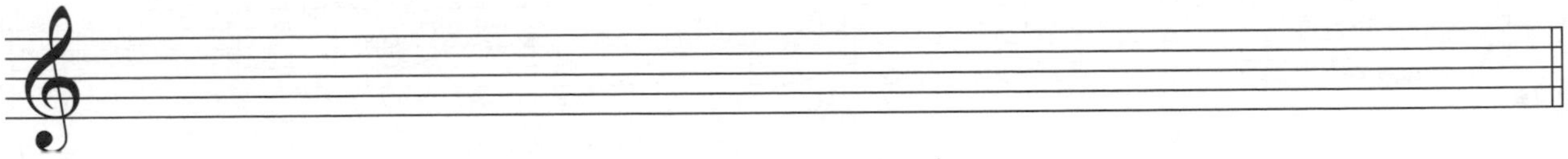

C# melodic minor in eighth notes

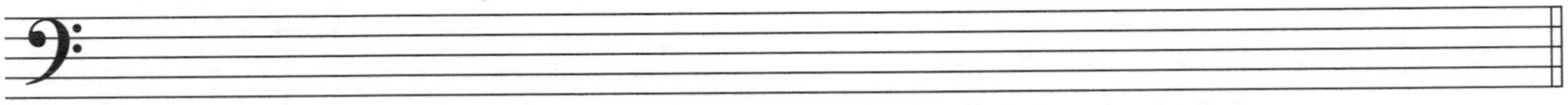

F natural minor in quarter notes

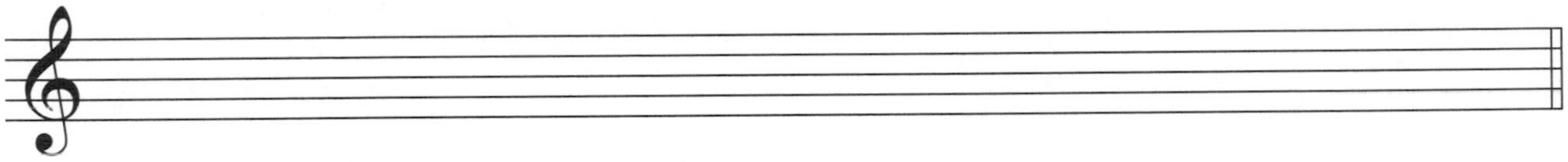

E melodic minor in whole notes

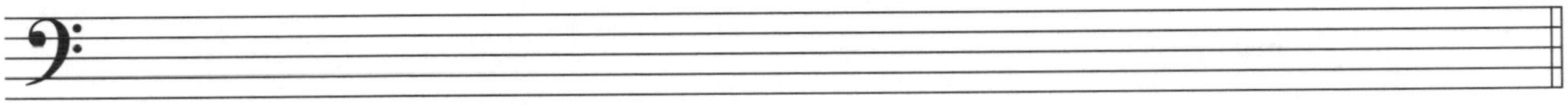

F# harmonic minor in sixteenth notes

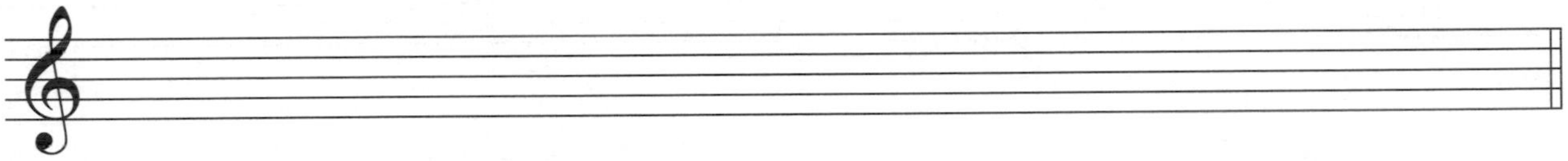

C melodic minor in dotted half notes

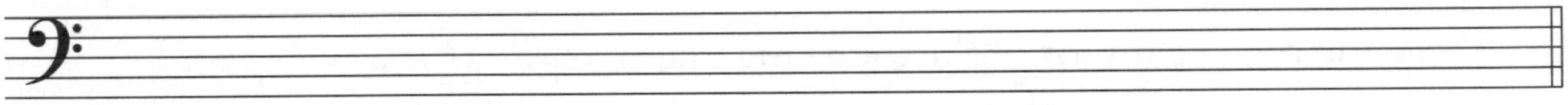

G# harmonic minor in sixteenth notes

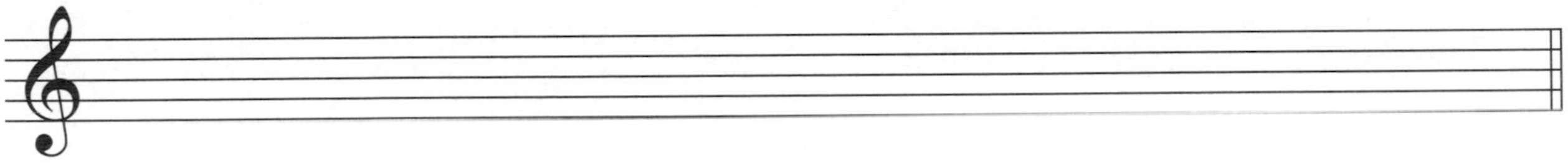

E♭ natural minor in whole notes

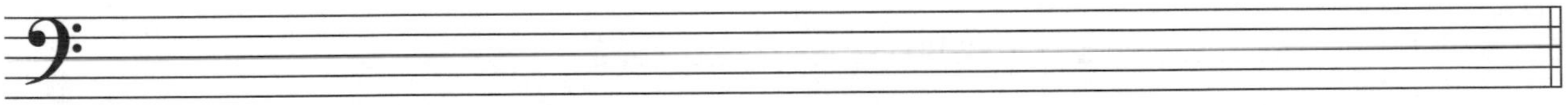

B melodic minor in dotted quarter notes

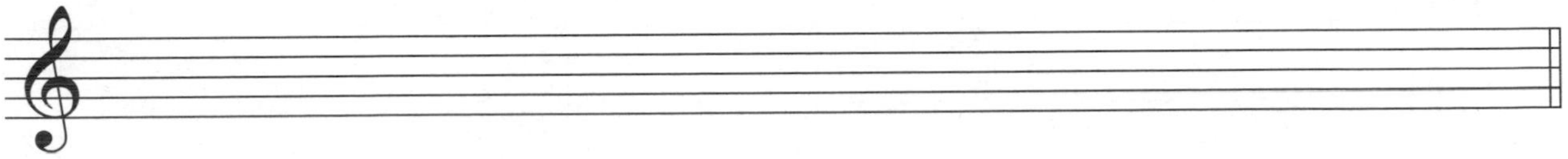

B♭ harmonic minor in eighth notes

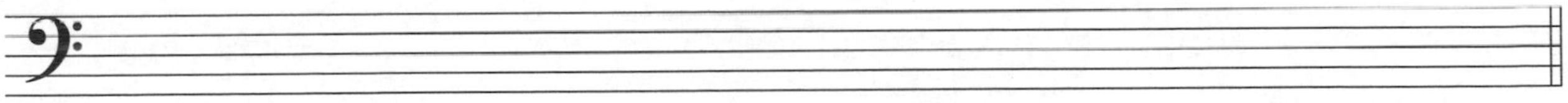

## MINOR SCALES

4. Name the minor keys for the following key signatures.

5. Name the relative minor of the following major keys.

F# major _____     B♭ major _____

G major _____      E♭ major _____

C# major _____     E major _____

A♭ major _____     D♭ major _____

C major _____      F major _____

B major _____      G♭ major _____

A major _____      C♭ major _____

D major _____

6.   Write the following scales, ascending and descending, using key signatures.

A major

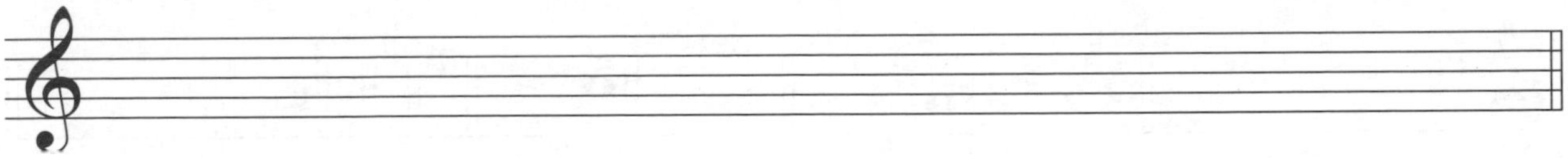

The relative melodic minor of A major

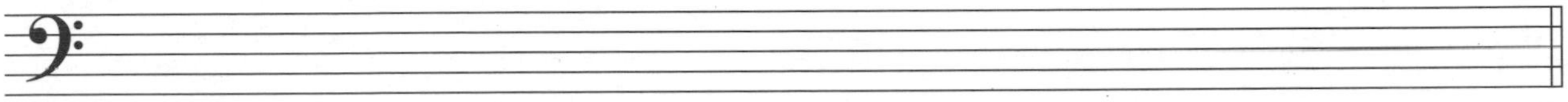

The tonic harmonic minor of A major

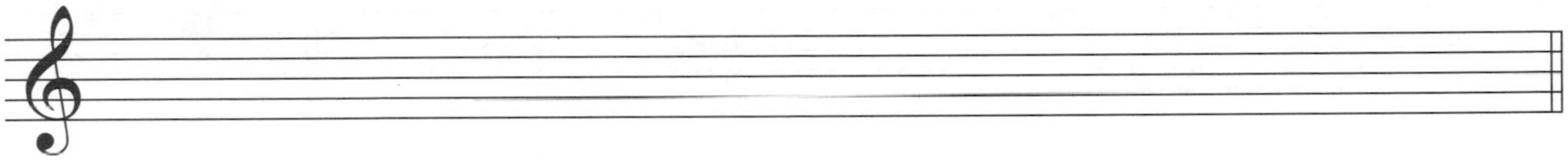

F♯ major from dominant to dominant

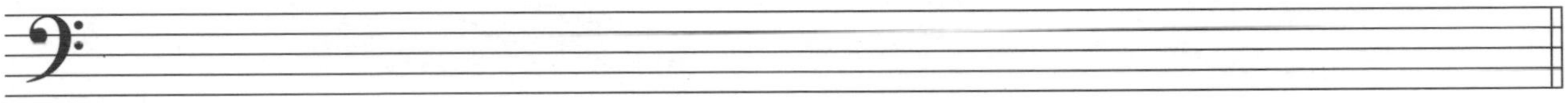

E♭ major from supertonic to supertonic

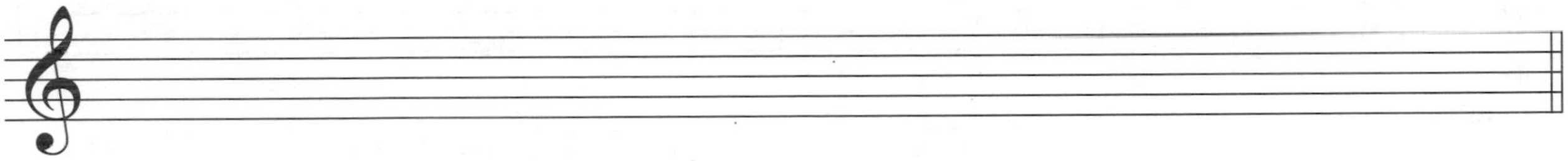

G harmonic minor from leading note to leading note

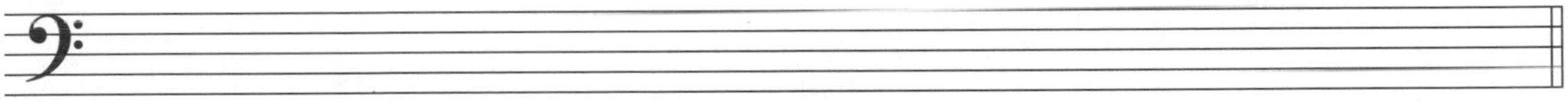

B♭ melodic minor

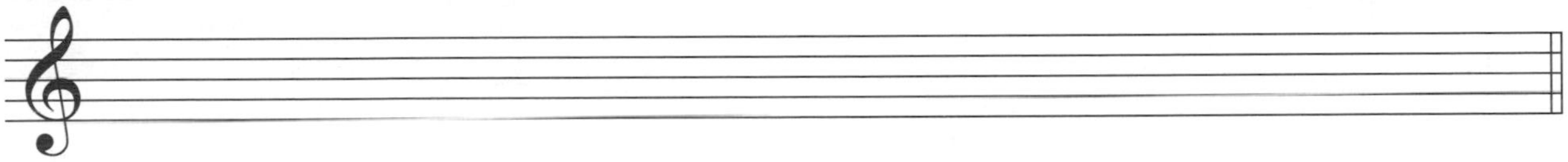

The tonic major of B♭ minor

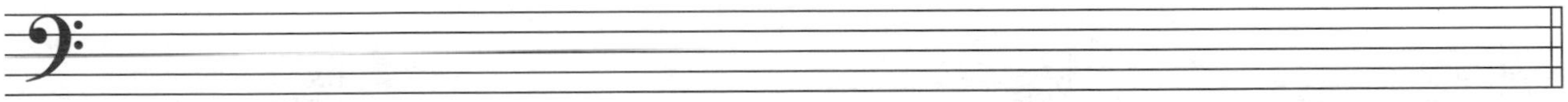

The relative harmonic minor of C♯ major from mediant to mediant

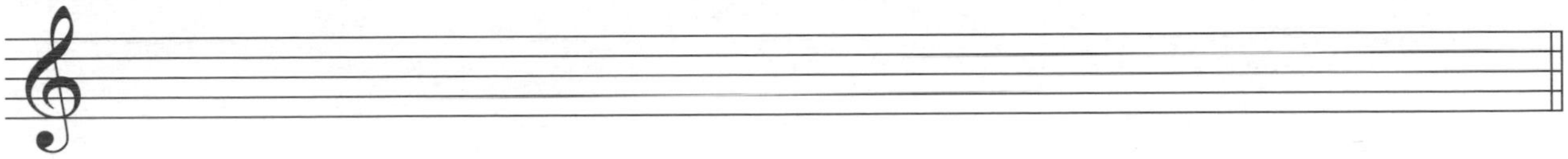

B major from subdominant to subdominant

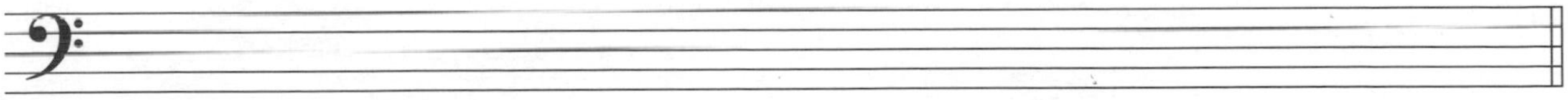

# MINOR SCALES

7. For the following notes, name the minor key and the degree of the scale (tonic, dominant, etc.).

key: _____   _____   _____   _____

degree: _____   _____   _____   _____

key: _____   _____   _____   _____

degree: _____   _____   _____   _____

key: _____   _____   _____   _____

degree: _____   _____   _____   _____

key: _____   _____   _____   _____

degree: _____   _____   _____   _____

key: _____   _____   _____   _____

degree: _____   _____   _____   _____

8. Write the following scales, ascending and descending, using accidentals instead of a key signature.

The relative harmonic minor of D♭ major

The tonic melodic minor of C major

F♯ natural minor from submediant to submediant

B harmonic minor from tonic to tonic

The melodic minor with G♯ as the dominant

The natural minor with E as the supertonic

G♭ major from mediant to mediant

C♯ major

The major scale with D♯ as the submediant

The major scale with G♯ as the leading note

## MINOR SCALES

9. Add clefs, key signatures, and any necessary accidentals to create the following scales.

F harmonic minor

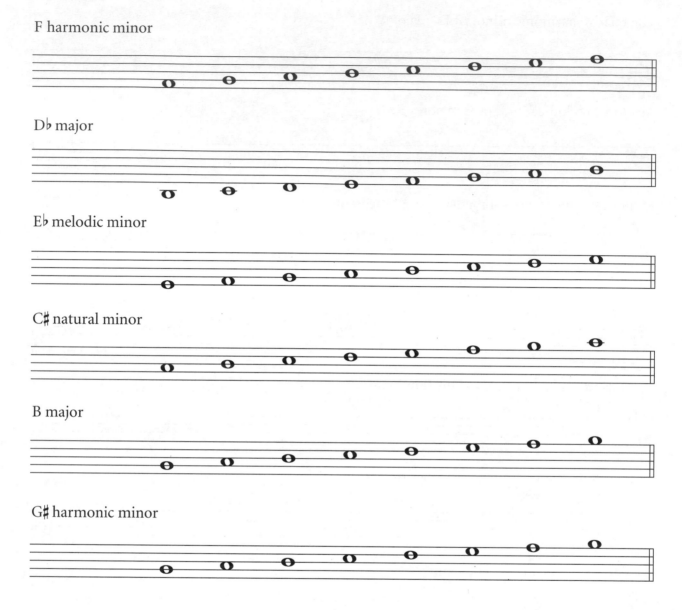

Db major

Eb melodic minor

C♯ natural minor

B major

G♯ harmonic minor

10. Learn the following Italian terms and their definitions.

| *animato* | lively, animated |
| *brillante* | brilliant |
| *con* | with |
| *con brio* | with vigor, spirit |
| *con espressione* | with expression |
| *espressivo* | expressive, with expression |
| *leggiero* | light, nimble, quick |
| *spiritoso* | spirited |
| *tranquillo* | quiet, tranquil |

1. Write the following scales in the tenor clef, ascending and descending, using key signatures.

C melodic minor

A♭ harmonic minor

The harmonic minor scale with a key signature of six sharps

B melodic minor from dominant to dominant

C♯ harmonic minor from mediant to mediant

The melodic minor scale with a key signature of six flats

F♯ melodic minor from submediant to submediant

B♭ harmonic minor

# MINOR SCALES

2.  Write the following scales in the alto clef, ascending and descending, using key signatures.

D melodic minor from subdominant to subdominant

G harmonic minor from leading note to leading note

The harmonic minor scale with a key signature of four flats

A melodic minor

B natural minor from supertonic to supertonic

The major scale with a key signature of seven sharps

G♯ melodic minor

A♯ harmonic minor

3.   Add clefs, key signatures, and any necessary accidentals to form the following scales.

D major

G♯ harmonic minor

F♯ major

G♭ major

F melodic minor

E harmonic minor

A major

B♭ melodic minor

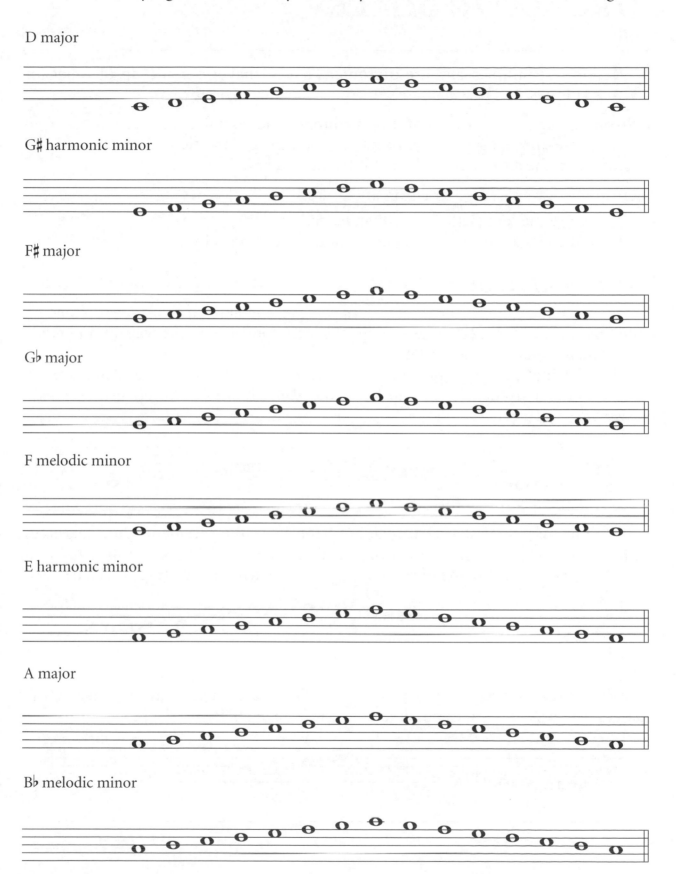

# CHROMATIC SCALES

**I A**

Major and minor scales are **diatonic**. That is, they are made up of tones and semitones, and they contain only notes that belong to the scale.

A **chromatic scale** is made up of only semitones and contains all twelve notes in the octave. There are two types of chromatic scales: the chromatic scale that has no key signature and the chromatic scale that is based on a key.

There are two simple rules for chromatic scales:

1. Never use the same letter more than twice.
2. Do not change the name of the tonic note enharmonically.

## CHROMATIC SCALES WITHOUT A KEY SIGNATURE

In this chromatic scale, the notes are *raised going up* and *lowered going down.* When you write this chromatic scale, you use sharps as soon as possible on the way up, and flats as soon as possible on the way down.
Here is a chromatic scale starting on C. Sharps are used on the way up, and flats are used on the way down. *Notice that the bar line in the middle cancels all the accidentals used on the way up.*

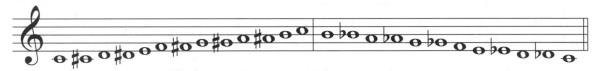

In the following scale (F sharp chromatic), all the descending accidentals are flats except the last note. Since F sharp is the starting note, F sharp must also be the final note. You cannot change the name of the starting note enharmonically (i.e., to G flat).

Here is a chromatic scale starting on D flat. This scale must begin with flats, but it changes to sharps as soon as possible on the way up. Flats are used all the way down.

1. Write the following scales, ascending and descending, using accidentals instead of a key signature.

Chromatic scale starting on E

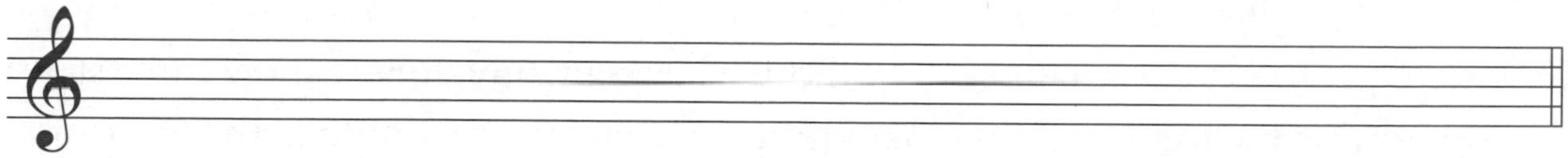

Chromatic scale starting on A♭

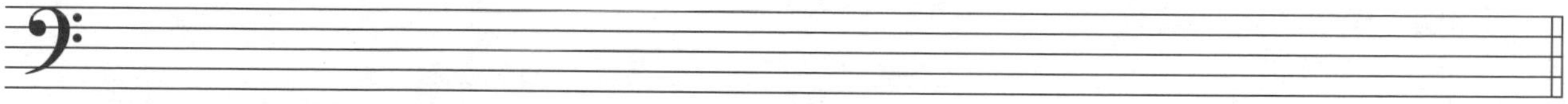

Chromatic scale starting on C♯

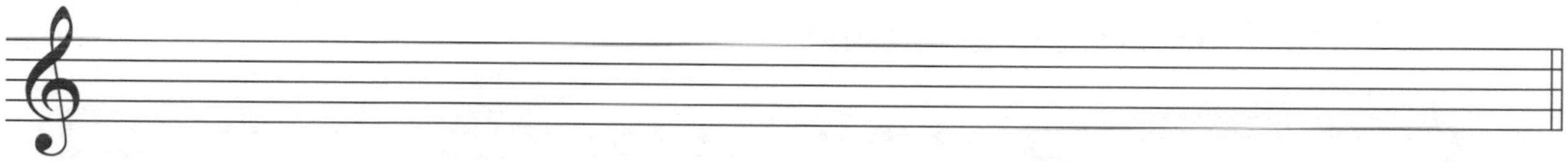

Chromatic scale starting on B♭

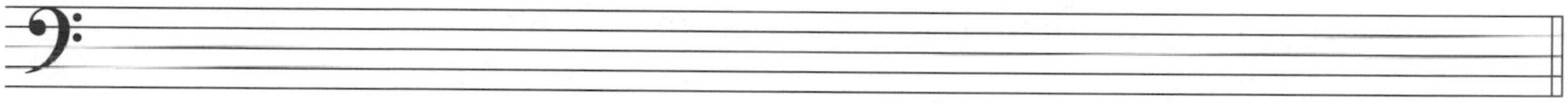

Chromatic scale starting on G

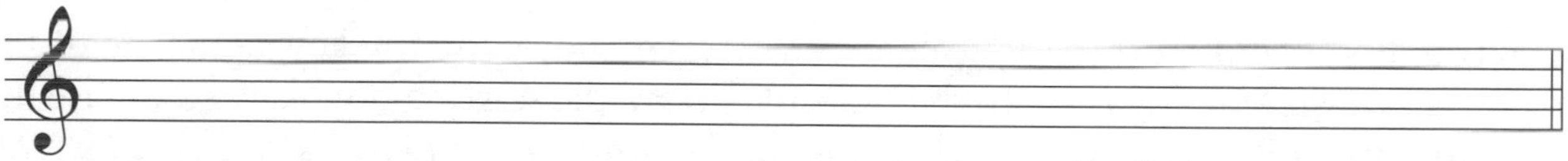

Chromatic scale starting on E♭

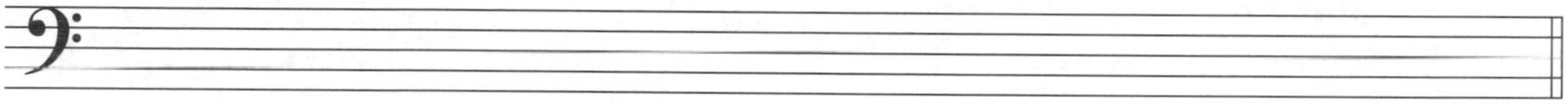

Chromatic scale starting on D

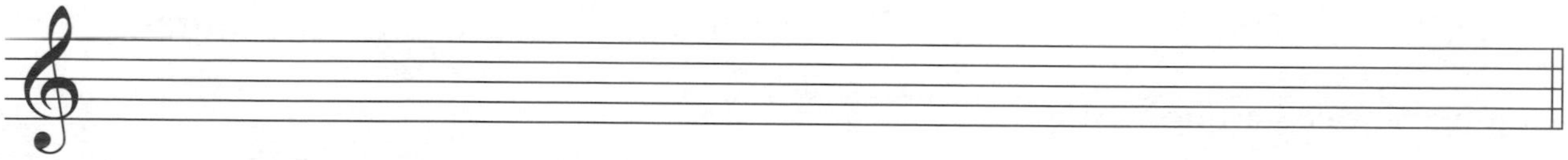

Chromatic scale starting on G♯

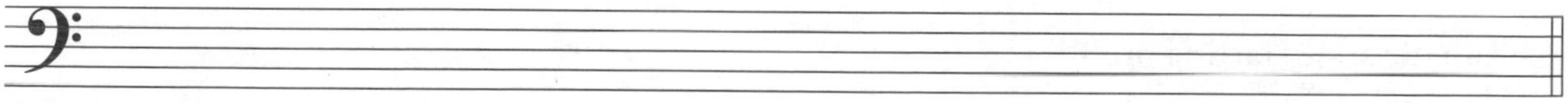

# *CHROMATIC SCALES BASED ON A KEY*

A chromatic scale may also be based on a major scale. This form of chromatic scale may be written with or without a key signature.

To write this type of chromatic scale without a key signature, follow these three steps:

1. Determine the tonic and dominant notes by using the first note as the tonic of a major scale. Write the tonic and dominant notes, ascending and descending.

   In the example below, the scale begins on E. The tonic and dominant notes of E major are E and B.

2. Write each of the remaining notes *twice.*

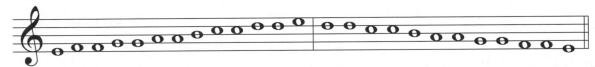

3. Add the necessary accidentals to form a chromatic scale.

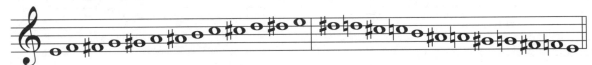

To write this type of chromatic scale with a key signature, use the key signature of the major key of the starting note. In the example below, the starting note is E, so we use the key signature of E major. *Note the difference in the pattern of accidentals between this scale and the one above that has no key signature.*

2. Write the following scales, ascending and descending, using key signatures.

Chromatic scale starting on F

Chromatic scale starting on B

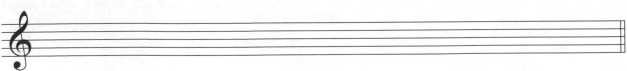

**I**
**A**

3. Write the following scales, ascending and descending, using key signatures.

Chromatic scale starting on E♭

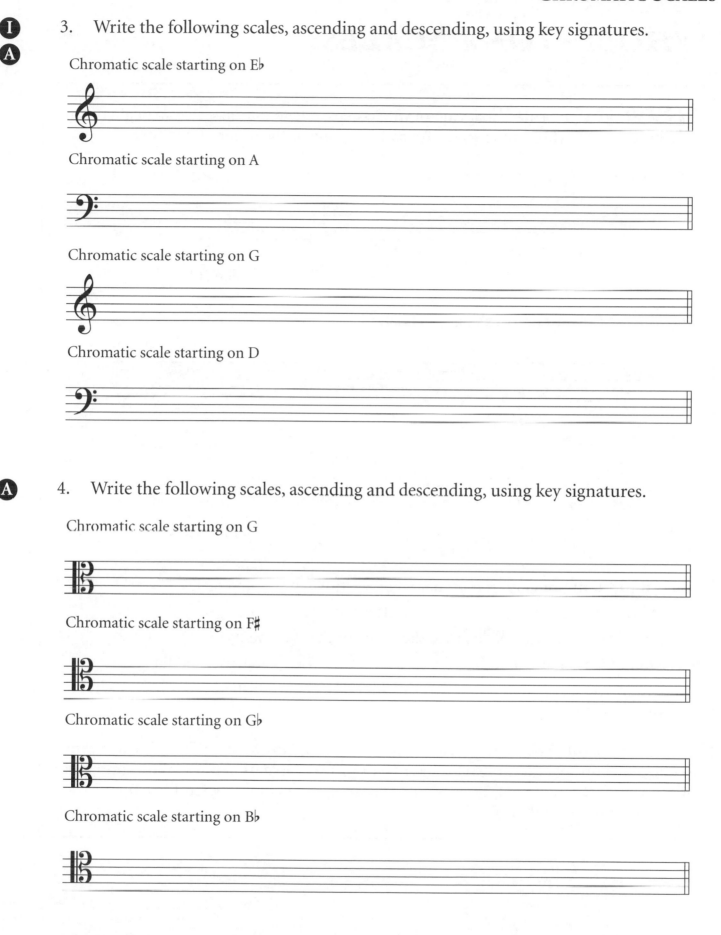

Chromatic scale starting on A

Chromatic scale starting on G

Chromatic scale starting on D

**A**

4. Write the following scales, ascending and descending, using key signatures.

Chromatic scale starting on G

Chromatic scale starting on F♯

Chromatic scale starting on G♭

Chromatic scale starting on B♭

# WHOLE-TONE SCALES

**I A**

The **whole-tone scale** is made up of whole steps. A whole-tone scale can begin on any note, but all whole-tone scales are based on one or the other of two forms.

One form starts on C.

dim 3rd

The other form starts on C sharp or D flat.

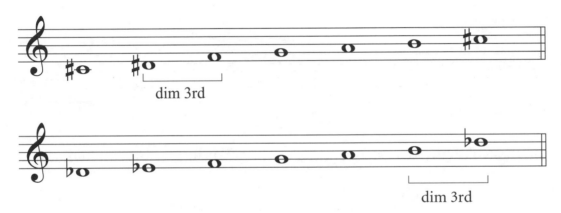

dim 3rd

dim 3rd

A few important points to remember when writing whole-tone scales:

- Whole-tone scales use six different letter names.
- Do not enharmonically change the name of the starting note.
- Do not mix sharps and flats in the same scale: use all sharps or all flats.
- Every whole-tone scale contains the interval of a diminished 3rd. (See the chapter on Intervals on p. 87.)

Since the notes of a whole-tone scale are spaced evenly, any note can function as a tonic. Music based on a whole-tone scale has a feeling of restlessness because of the ambiguity of the tonic. A number of 20th-century composers, including Claude Debussy, used whole-tone scales in their music.

1.   Add accidentals to the following to create whole-tone scales.

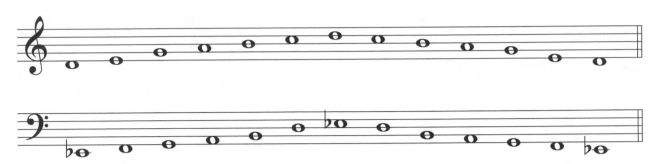

The following excerpt is an example of a composition based on the whole-tone scale. Here, the composer has used notes from the whole-tone scale beginning on C to create the melody.

Write and play the whole-tone scale that this piece is based on, ascending and descending, and then play the excerpt from *Starfish at Night*. Listen carefully. What sort of mood is created by the composer's use of whole tones?

Whole-tone scale starting on C

## Starfish at Night

Anne Crosby
(b. 1968)

Source: *Freddie the Frog*
© Copyright 1997 The Frederick Harris Music Co., Limited, Mississauga, Ontario, Canada.

# WHOLE-TONE SCALES

1.  Write the following whole-tone scales, ascending and descending.

The whole-tone scale starting on F

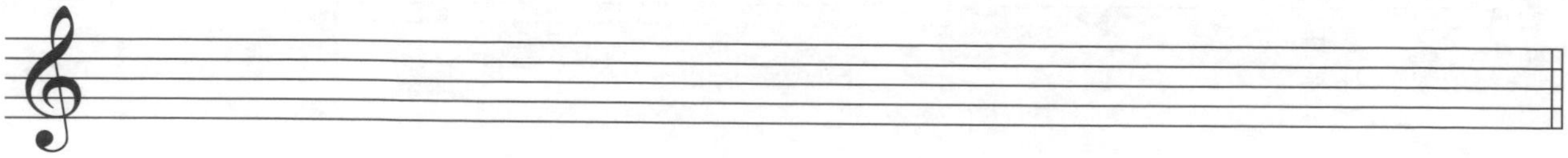

The whole-tone scale starting on D♯

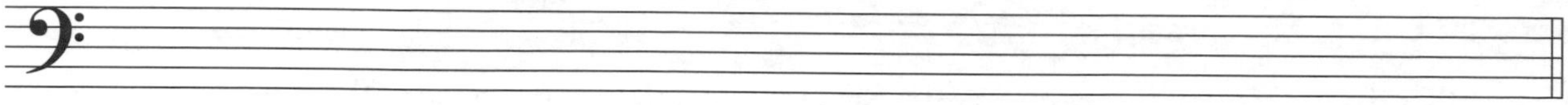

The whole-tone scale starting on E♭

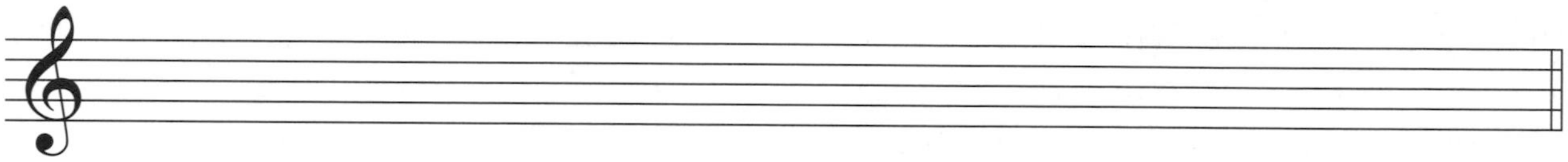

The whole-tone scale starting on A

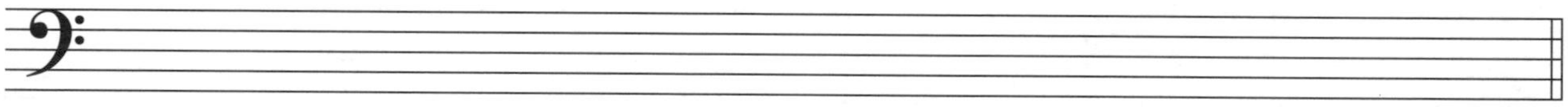

# PENTATONIC SCALES

**Ⓘ**
**Ⓐ**

The **pentatonic scale** consists of five notes, and is one of the oldest scales in existence. It was found in Asian music as early as 2000 B.C., and is common in folk music. Pentatonic scales were also used by some composers in the 19th and 20th centuries. We will study two types of pentatonic scales.

The **major pentatonic scale** can be formed by removing the fourth and seventh degrees from a major scale.

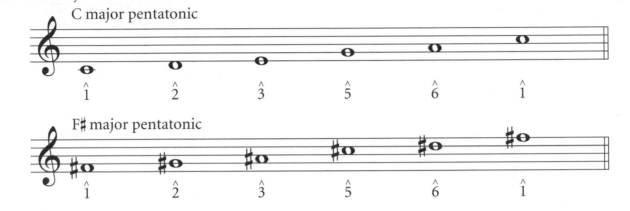

The melody in the following composition is based on the E flat major pentatonic scale. Write the E flat major pentatonic scale on the staff below, ascending and descending. Play *Bashkir Chastushka* and listen carefully for the pentatonic melody.

E♭ major pentatonic

## Bashkir Chastushka

Vladimir Blok
(1932–1996)

Source: *Twelve Pieces in Folk Modes*

# PENTATONIC SCALES

**I**
**A**

1. Write the following major pentatonic scales, ascending only.

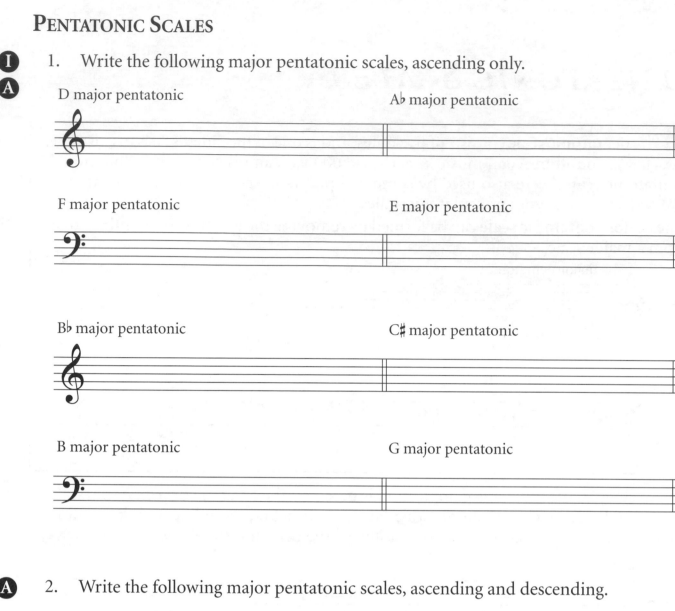

D major pentatonic

A♭ major pentatonic

F major pentatonic

E major pentatonic

B♭ major pentatonic

C♯ major pentatonic

B major pentatonic

G major pentatonic

**A**

2. Write the following major pentatonic scales, ascending and descending.

D♭ major pentatonic

E♭ major pentatonic

A major pentatonic

The **minor pentatonic scale** can be formed by removing the second and sixth degrees from a natural minor scale. The minor pentatonic scale always begins with the interval of a minor 3rd.

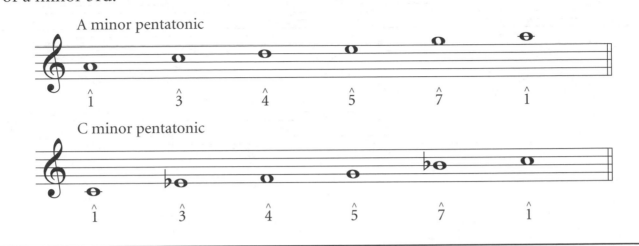

The following folk melody is based on the E minor pentatonic scale. Write the E minor pentatonic scale on the staff below, ascending and descending. Play *Land of the Silver Birch* and listen carefully for the pentatonic melody.

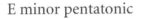

## Land of the Silver Birch

Folk melody

# PENTATONIC SCALES

**I**
**A**   1.   Write the following minor pentatonic scales, ascending and descending.

G minor pentatonic

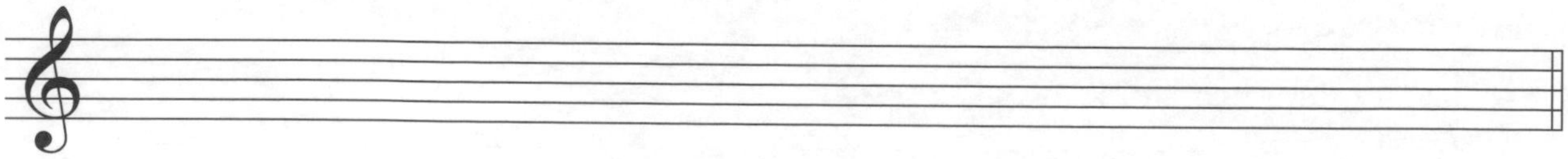

D minor pentatonic

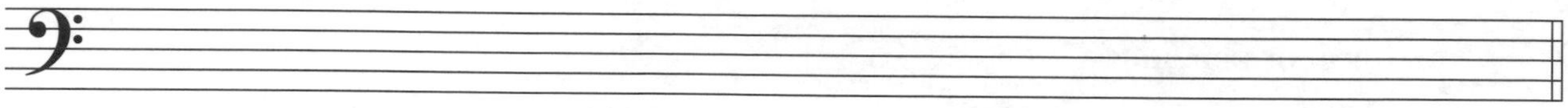

F minor pentatonic

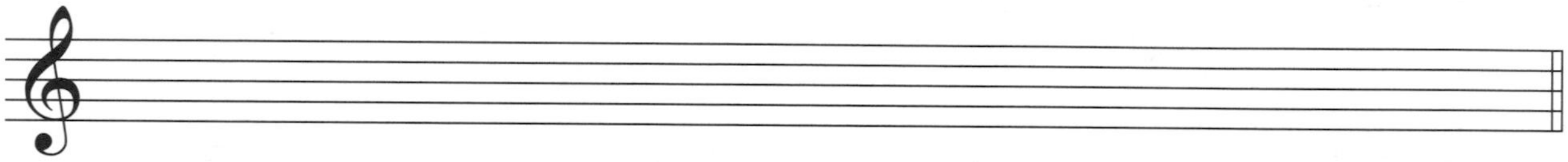

B minor pentatonic

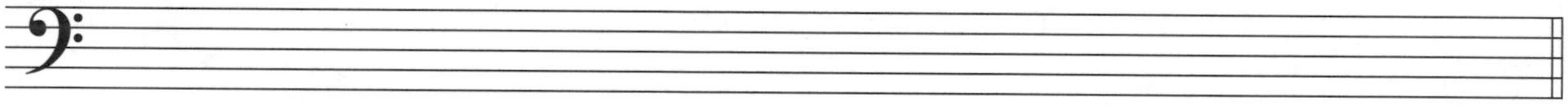

**A**   2.   Write the following pentatonic scales, ascending and descending.

C minor pentatonic

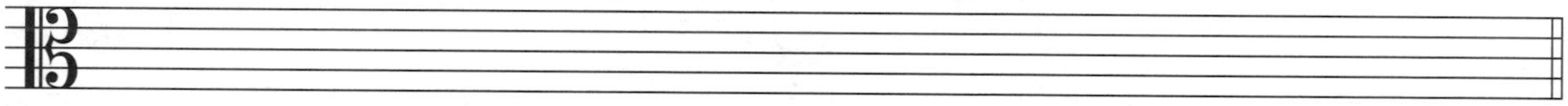

A major pentatonic

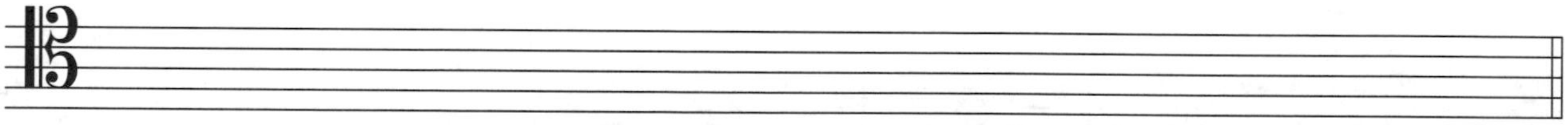

A minor pentatonic

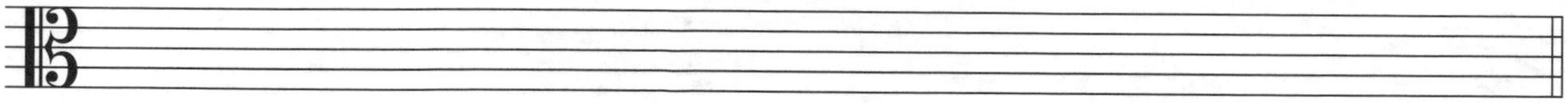

B♭ major pentatonic

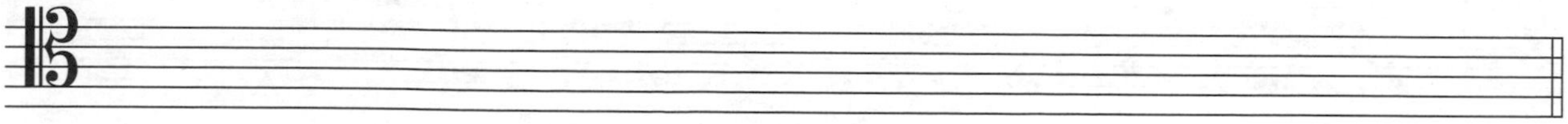

# THE BLUES SCALE

**I**
**A**

Blues is an African American music genre characterized by a scale in which certain notes are lowered. A blues tune is usually twelve measures long and consists of three four-measure phrases.

Here is a basic blues scale:

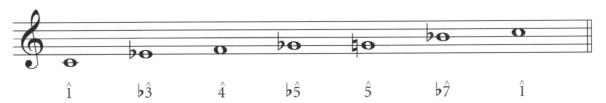

If you compare this scale to a major scale, you will find three differences:

1. The second and sixth degree are missing.

2. The third, fifth, and seventh degrees are lowered by a semitone—these are called "blue" notes.

3. The fifth degree of the scale occurs twice (once unaltered and once lowered).

A blues scale can be formed from a major scale by omitting the second and sixth degrees and lowering the third, fifth and seventh degrees.

1. Write the following blues scales, ascending only.

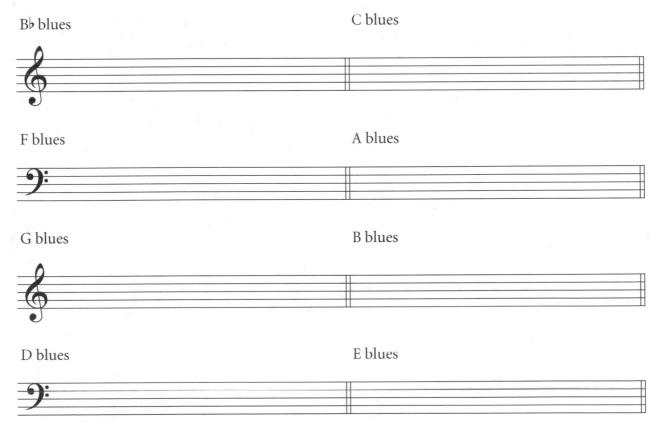

## THE BLUES SCALE

The following piece is an example of the blues in C. The melody of *Cool Blue* is made up of notes from the C blues scale. Practice the C blues scale and then play *Cool Blue*. Try playing in swing time. This means playing the eighth notes as if they were a triplet consisting of a quarter and an eighth note.

Using the same left-hand bass part and the C blues scale, improvise your own blues. Use different rhythms and make up your own patterns.

## Cool Blue

Mark Sarnecki

# THE OCTATONIC SCALE

**I**
**A**

The **octatonic** scale is an eight-note scale in which tones and semitones alternate. Octatonic scales are sometimes called **diminished** scales. This scale is used prominently in the music of several composers, including Nicolai Rimsky-Korsakov, Igor Stravinsky, and Béla Bartók. It begins and ends on the same note, so like all scales, the tonic must not be changed enharmonically. This scale can begin with either a tone or a semitone. Only three transpositions of the octatonic scale are possible. An octatonic scale starting on any note will have the same combination of pitches as one of the three scales shown below.

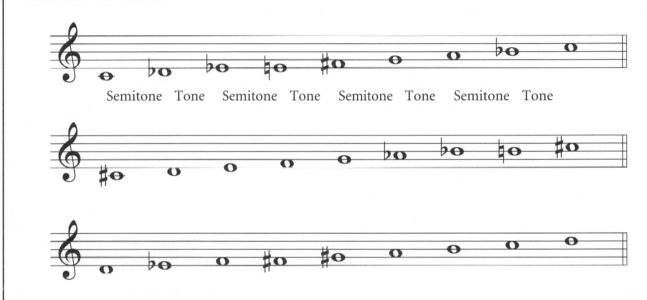

Semitone   Tone   Semitone   Tone   Semitone   Tone   Semitone   Tone

1.   Write the following octatonic scales, ascending and descending.

On F, start with a tone

On B, start with a semitone

On D, start with a tone

## The Octatonic Scale

On E, start with a semitone

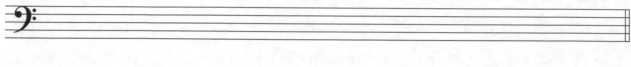

On A, start with a semitone

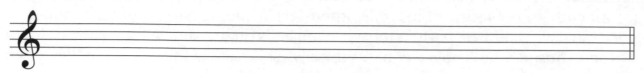

# MODES

A

Broadly speaking, a mode is a pattern of notes arranged in a scale. Major and minor scales are only two examples of modes. The scales, or modes, below are called **church modes**—a system of modes that became established during the Middle Ages and played an important role in the composition of Gregorian chant. The origins of this system, however, date back to ancient Greek theory.

Each mode has its own pattern of tones and semitones. The versions here can be played using only the white keys of the piano, and they are named for the starting note followed by the name of the mode (for example, D Dorian).

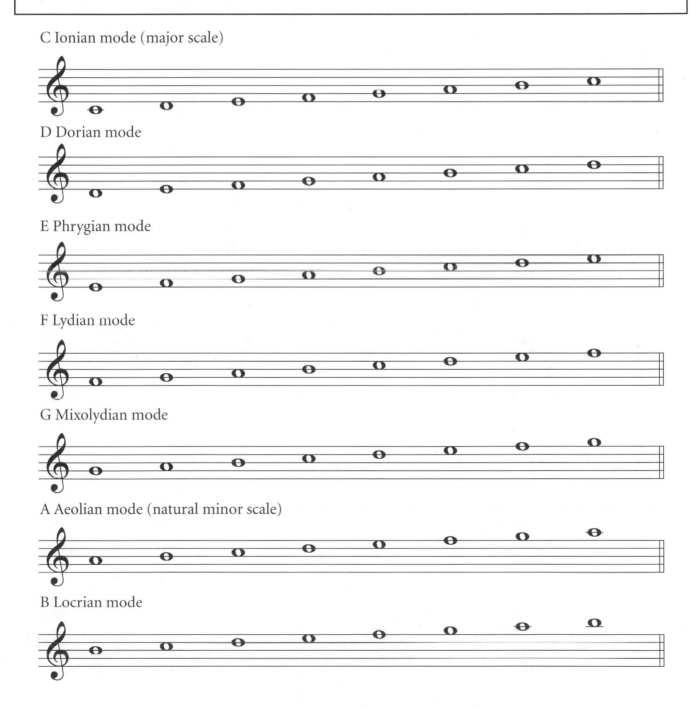

C Ionian mode (major scale)

D Dorian mode

E Phrygian mode

F Lydian mode

G Mixolydian mode

A Aeolian mode (natural minor scale)

B Locrian mode

## MODES

The easiest way to write these church modes is to derive them from the pattern of tones and semitones in a major scale. The following examples show a number of modal scales starting on the note G.

### Ionian Mode

The Ionian mode has the same pattern of tones and semitones as a major scale. To write the G Ionian mode, build a major scale on G.

The G major scale has one sharp (F sharp) in its key signature. To write the G Ionian mode, use F sharp as an accidental.

G Ionian

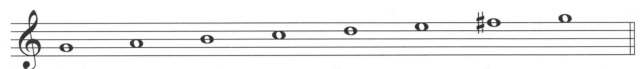

### Dorian Mode

The Dorian mode has the same pattern of tones and semitones as a major scale starting on its *second* degree.

G is the second degree of the F major scale. F major has one flat (B flat) in its key signature. To write the G Dorian mode, start on G but use B flat as an accidental.

F major

G Dorian

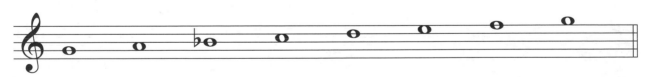

*The Complete Elementary Music Rudiments*

## Phrygian Mode

The Phrygian mode has the same pattern of tones and semitones as a major scale starting on its *third* degree.

G is the third degree of the E flat major scale. E flat major has three flats (B flat, E flat, A flat) in its key signature. To write the G Phrygian mode, start on G but use B flat, E flat, and A flat as accidentals.

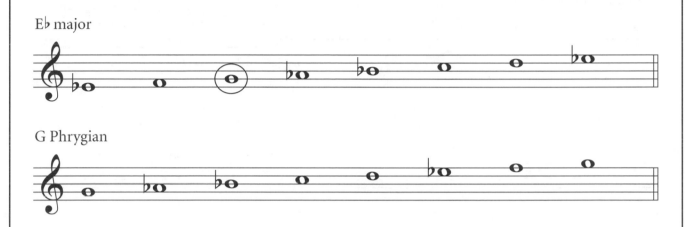

E♭ major

G Phrygian

## Lydian Mode

The Lydian mode has the same pattern of tones and semitones as a major scale starting on its *fourth* degree.

G is the fourth degree of the D major scale. D major has two sharps (F sharp, C sharp) in its key signature. To write the G Lydian mode, start on G but use F sharp and C sharp as accidentals.

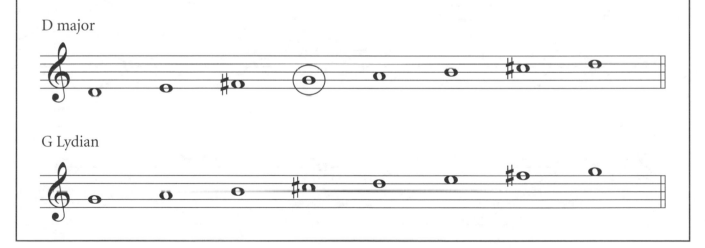

D major

G Lydian

# MODES

## Mixolydian Mode

The Mixolydian mode has the same pattern of tones and semitones as a major scale starting on its *fifth* degree.

G is the fifth degree of the C major scale. C major has no sharps or flats in its key signature. To write the G Mixolydian mode, start on G but do not use any accidentals.

C major

G Mixolydian

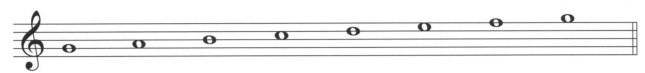

## Aeolian Mode

The Aeolian mode has the same pattern of tones and semitones as a major scale starting on its *sixth* degree—it has the same pattern as a natural minor scale.

G is the sixth degree of the B flat major scale. B flat major has two flats (B flat, E flat) in its key signature. To write the G Aeolian mode, start on G but use B flat and E flat as accidentals.

B♭ major

G Aeolian

*The Complete Elementary Music Rudiments*

**Locrian Mode**

The Locrian mode has the same pattern of tones and semitones as a major scale starting on its *seventh* degree.

G is the seventh degree of the A flat major scale. A flat major has four flats (B flat, E flat, A flat, D flat) in its key signature. To write the G Locrian mode, start on G but use B flat, E flat, A flat, and D flat as accidentals.

A♭ major

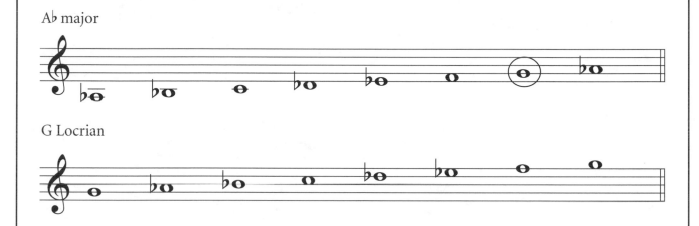

G Locrian

**A**

**How to Identify a Mode**

To identify the mode of a scale, follow these three steps:

1.  Collect all the accidentals and determine the major key.

    The scale in the example below has two flats: B flat and E flat. These are the two flats in the key signature of B flat major.

2.  Look at the starting note. Determine the scale degree of this note in the major scale for the key signature.

    The scale starts on C. C is the second degree of B flat major scale.

3.  Determine which mode has the same pattern of tones and semitones as the major scale that starts on that scale degree.

    The Dorian mode has the same pattern of tones and semitones as a major scale that begins on its second degree. Therefore, this is the C Dorian mode.

Many folk melodies are based on modes. The melody in the following composition uses the C Mixolydian mode. Write the C Mixolydian mode on the staff below. Play *In Hungarian Style*, listening carefully to the character and mood of this piece.

C Mixolydian

## In Hungarian Style

Vladimir Blok
(1932–1996)

Allegretto, alla burla

Source: *Twelve Pieces in Folk Modes*
© Copyright 1995 The Frederick Harris Music Co., Limited, Mississauga, Ontario, Canada.

1. Write the following modal scales, ascending only.

E Mixolydian

D Dorian

C Aeolian

A♭ Lydian

B Locrian

2. Identify the following modal scales.

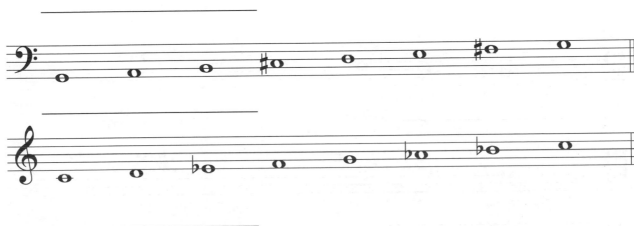

## MODES

3. Write the following modal scales, ascending and descending.

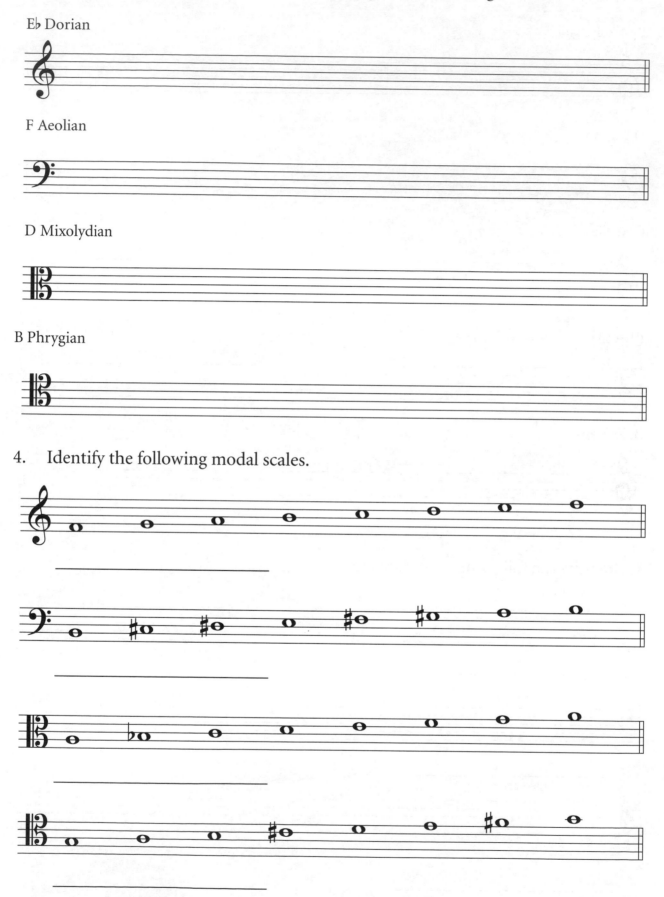

Eb Dorian

F Aeolian

D Mixolydian

B Phrygian

4. Identify the following modal scales.

# IDENTIFYING SCALES

1. Name each of the following scales as major, natural minor, harmonic minor, melodic minor, whole-tone, major pentatonic, minor pentatonic, chromatic, blues, or octatonic.

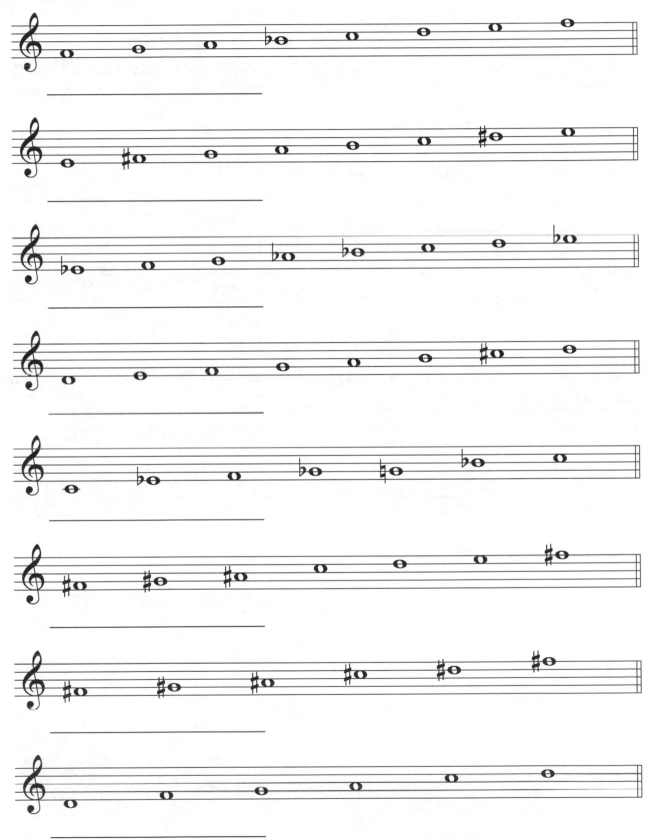

## IDENTIFYING SCALES

2. Name each of the following scales as major, natural minor, harmonic minor, melodic minor, whole-tone, major pentatonic, minor pentatonic, chromatic, blues, or octatonic.

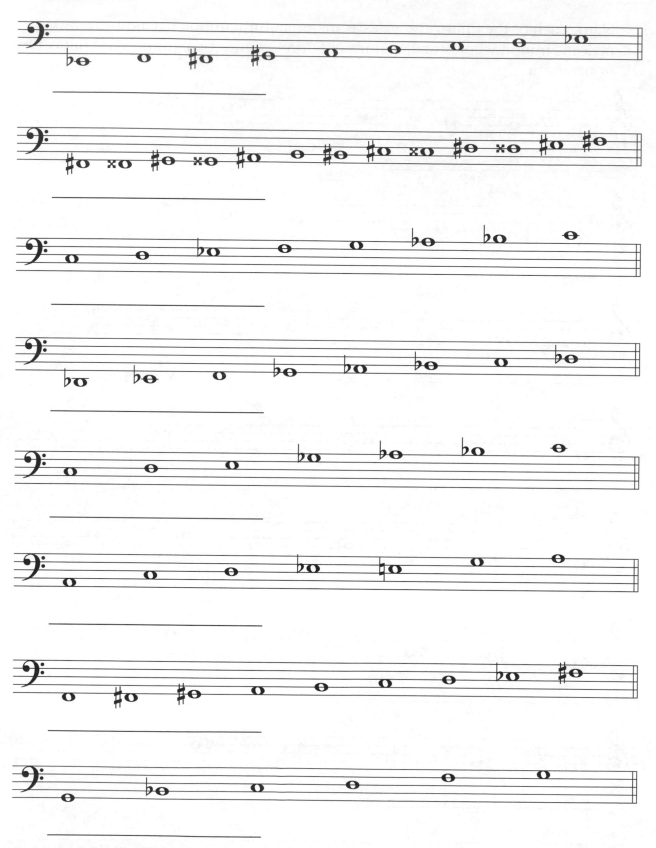

**A** 3. Name each of the following scales as major, natural minor, harmonic minor, melodic minor, whole-tone, major pentatonic, minor pentatonic, chromatic, blues, or octatonic.

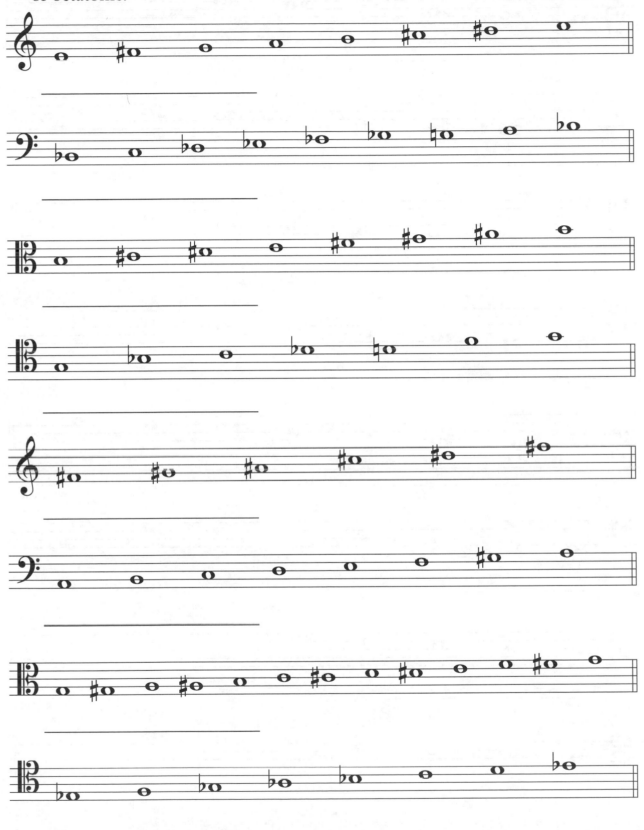

## IDENTIFYING SCALES

4. Identify the following modes.

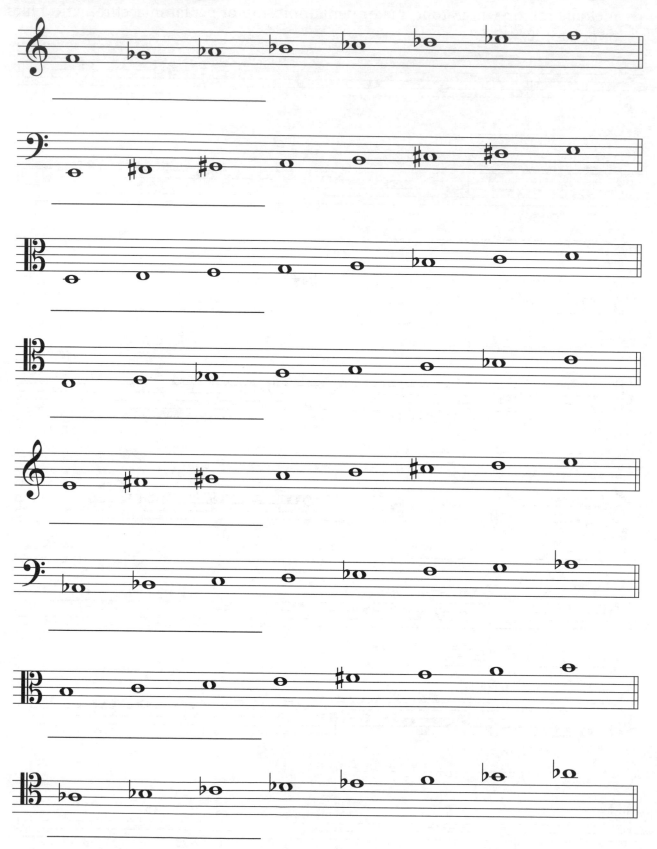

# INTERVALS

An **interval** is the distance between two notes. When the notes of an interval are played one after the other, the interval is called **melodic**.

When the notes of an interval are played at the same time, the interval is called **harmonic**.

All intervals have a specific number. This number is determined by counting the letter names of the notes in the interval from the lowest to the highest.

There are five letter names from C to G.

C D E F G
1 2 3 4 5

This is an interval of a 5th.

1. Name the following melodic intervals.

____  ____  ____  ____  ____  ____  ____  ____

2. Name the following harmonic intervals.

____  ____  ____  ____  ____  ____  ____  ____

3. Write the following intervals above the given notes.

8    6    3    4    7    5    2    8    6    2

## INTERVALS

The following intervals are formed between the notes of the major scale.

| perfect unison | major 2nd | major 3rd | perfect 4th | perfect 5th | major 6th | major 7th | perfect 8ve |

The intervals of a unison, 4th, 5th, and octave are classified as **perfect intervals.** The abbreviation for a perfect interval is "per"—for example, per 4.

The intervals of a 2nd, 3rd, 6th, and 7th are classified as **major intervals.** The abbreviation for a major interval is "maj"—for example, maj 3.

Think of the bottom note of an interval as the tonic of a major scale.

If the upper note of the interval is a member the scale of the lower note, the interval will be either perfect or major. For example, D to F sharp is a major 3rd because F sharp is the third note of the D major scale. F to B flat is a perfect fourth because B flat is the fourth note of the F major scale.

4.  Write the scale of D major, ascending and descending, using accidentals instead of a key signature.

5.  Write the following intervals above the note D.

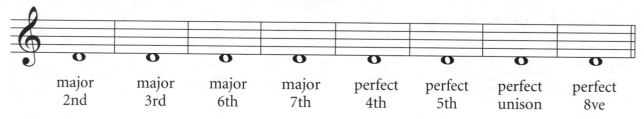

| major 2nd | major 3rd | major 6th | major 7th | perfect 4th | perfect 5th | perfect unison | perfect 8ve |

6.  Write the scale of A flat major, ascending and descending, using accidentals instead of a key signature.

7.  Write the following intervals above the note A flat.

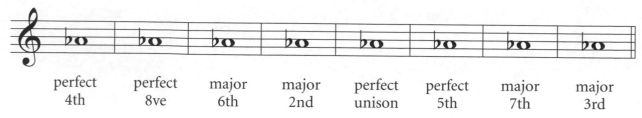

| perfect 4th | perfect 8ve | major 6th | major 2nd | perfect unison | perfect 5th | major 7th | major 3rd |

8. Write the scale of E major, ascending and descending, using accidentals instead of a key signature.

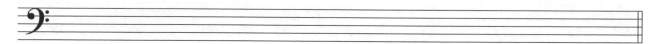

9. Write the following intervals above the note E.

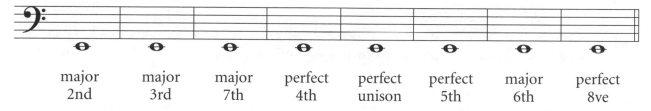

| major 2nd | major 3rd | major 7th | perfect 4th | perfect unison | perfect 5th | major 6th | perfect 8ve |

A **minor interval** is one semitone smaller than a major interval. In other words, the notes of a minor interval are *one semitone closer together* than the notes of a major interval.

Only 2nds, 3rds, 6ths, and 7ths can be minor intervals.

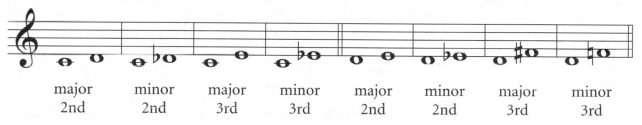

| major 2nd | minor 2nd | major 3rd | minor 3rd | major 2nd | minor 2nd | major 3rd | minor 3rd |

The abbreviation for a minor interval is "min"—for example, min 3.

To determine if an interval is major or minor, think of the bottom note as the tonic of a major scale. If the top note is a member of the major scale of the bottom note, the interval is major. If the top note is a semitone lower, the interval is minor.

For example, D to F natural is a 3rd, but F natural is not part of the scale of D major. The interval of D to F natural is one semitone smaller than the major 3rd of D to F sharp. This makes D to F natural a minor 3rd.

Intervals are always identified by using the lowest note as the tonic. This applies to melodic intervals, even when the lowest note comes after the highest note.

Eb to C
maj 6

F to A
maj 3

C to Bb
min 7

## INTERVALS

**B** **I** **A**   1.   Write the following intervals above the given notes.

per 8    maj 3    min 3    maj 6    min 6    per 5    maj 2    min 2

per 8    maj 3    min 3    maj 6    min 6    per 5    maj 2    min 2

per 8    maj 3    min 3    maj 6    min 6    per 5    maj 2    min 2

per 8    maj 3    min 3    maj 6    min 6    per 5    maj 2    min 2

per 8    maj 3    min 3    maj 6    min 6    per 5    maj 2    min 2

2.   Name the following intervals.

_____   _____   _____   _____   _____   _____   _____

_____   _____   _____   _____   _____   _____   _____

_____   _____   _____   _____   _____   _____   _____

3.  Name the following intervals.

4.  Write the following intervals above the given notes.

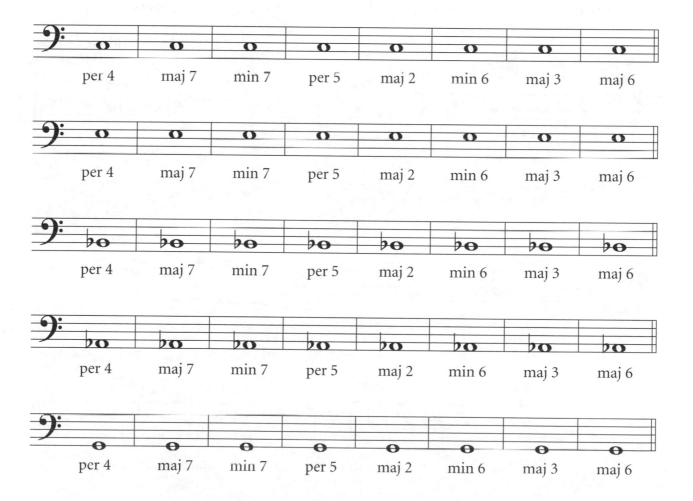

## INTERVALS

5.  Name the following intervals.

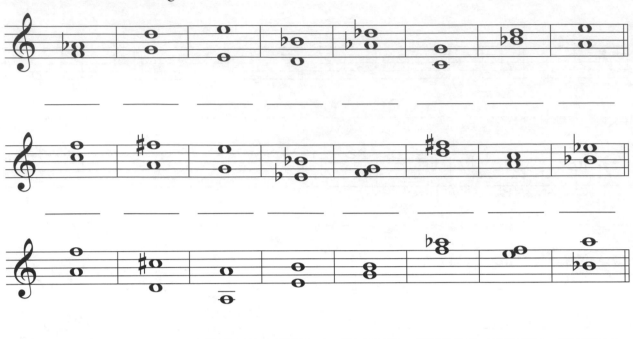

6.  Name the melodic intervals formed by the notes under the brackets.

Richard Wagner
(1813–1883)

Robert Schumann
(1810–1856)

Franz Joseph Haydn
(1732–1809)

*THE COMPLETE ELEMENTARY MUSIC RUDIMENTS*

An **augmented interval** is *one semitone larger than* a *perfect* or a *major* interval. In other words, the notes of an augmented interval are one semitone further apart than the notes of a perfect or major interval. A perfect or major interval can be made augmented by raising the top note or lowering the bottom note by *one semitone*. The abbreviation for an augmented interval is "aug"—for example, aug 4.

A **diminished interval** is *one semitone smaller than* either a *perfect* or a *minor* interval. In other words, the notes of a diminished interval are one semitone closer together than the notes of either a perfect interval or a minor interval. A perfect interval can be made diminished by lowering the top note or raising the bottom note by *one semitone*. The abbreviation for a diminished interval is "dim"—for example, dim 5.

Another name for the diminished 5th and its enharmonic equivalent, the augmented 4th, is the **tritone**. This name is derived from the fact that these intervals consist of three whole tones. The tritone is a difficult interval to sing and is often avoided when composing vocal music. At one time this interval was considered so dissonant or disagreeable it was called "*diabolus in musica*" or "the devil in music."

A minor interval can be made dimished by lowering the top note or raising the bottom note by *one semitone*.

Note that a diminished interval is *one semitone smaller than a perfect interval*, but *two semitones smaller than a major interval*.

# INTERVALS

Here is a summary of the relationship between the various types of intervals. The starting point is the note in the major scale.

| MINUS ← two semitones | MINUS ← one semitone | Note in the MAJOR SCALE | → PLUS one semitone |
|---|---|---|---|
| | **Diminished** unison, 4th, 5th, 8ᵛᵉ | **Perfect** unison, 4th, 5th, 8ᵛᵉ | **Augmented** unison, 4th, 5th, 8ᵛᵉ |
| **Diminished** 2nd, 3rd, 6th, 7th | **Minor** 2nd, 3rd, 6th, 7th | **Major** 2nd, 3rd, 6th, 7th | **Augmented** 2nd, 3rd, 6th, 7th |

1. Name the following intervals, then rewrite each as an augmented interval by changing the upper note.

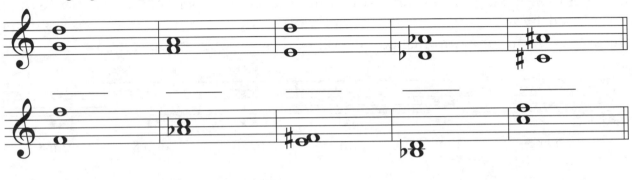

2. Name the following intervals, then rewrite each as an augmented interval by changing the bottom note.

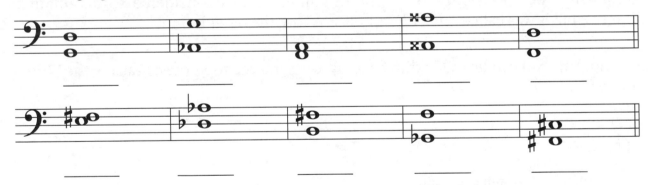

3. Name the following intervals, then rewrite each as an diminished interval by changing the top note.

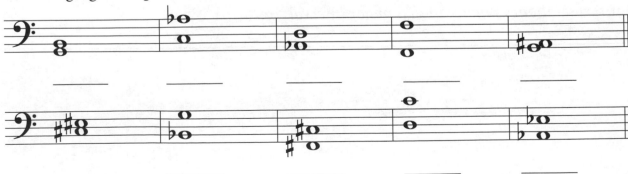

4. Name the following intervals, then rewrite each as an diminished interval by changing the bottom note.

5. Write the following intervals above the given notes.

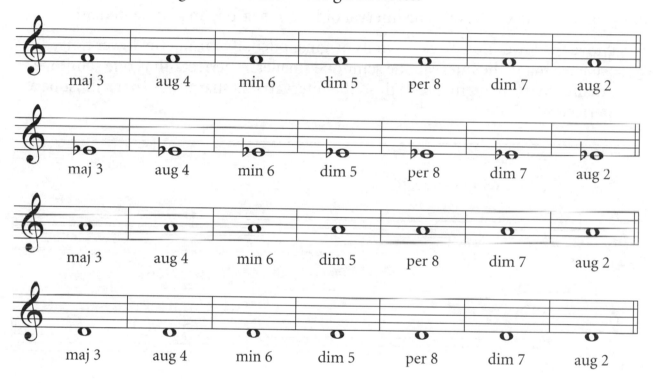

maj 3    aug 4    min 6    dim 5    per 8    dim 7    aug 2

maj 3    aug 4    min 6    dim 5    per 8    dim 7    aug 2

maj 3    aug 4    min 6    dim 5    per 8    dim 7    aug 2

maj 3    aug 4    min 6    dim 5    per 8    dim 7    aug 2

# INTERVALS

Sometimes the lowest note of an interval is not the tonic of a major key. For instance, in the example below, we know that D sharp to A sharp is a 5th, but there is no such key as D sharp major.

In order to name the interval, we must follow three steps:

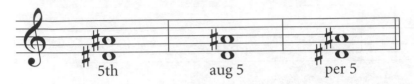

1. Lower the bottom note to one that is the tonic of an existing key. *Notice that this note has the same letter name, so the number of the interval remains the same.* In the example above, we lowered D sharp one semitone to D.

2. Name the new interval. The interval of D to A sharp is an augmented 5th.

3. Move the lower note back up to its original pitch. By raising the lower note, we have made the interval one semitone smaller. A perfect 5th is one semitone smaller than an augmented 5th so the interval of D sharp to A sharp must be a perfect 5th.

1. Name the following intervals.

### Inversion

When an interval is turned upside down, it is **inverted**. For example, when the interval of G to B is inverted, it becomes B to G.

There are two ways to invert an interval:

1. Write the lower note above the upper note.
2. Write the upper note belove the lower note.

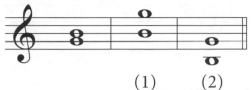

(1) (2)

When an interval is inverted:

| | | |
|---|---|---|
| **major** | becomes | **minor** |
| **minor** | becomes | **major** |
| **augmented** | becomes | **diminished** |
| **diminished** | becomes | **augmented** |
| **perfect** | remains | **perfect** |

maj 3 min 6   per 5 per 4   maj 2 min 7   dim 5 aug 4   aug 7   dim 2 maj 6 min 3   dim 3 aug 6 dim 8   aug 1

Note that the number of an interval *plus* the number of its inversion always equals *nine*.

2. Name the following intervals. Invert them and name the inversion.

3. Write the following intervals above the given notes. Invert each interval and name the inversion.

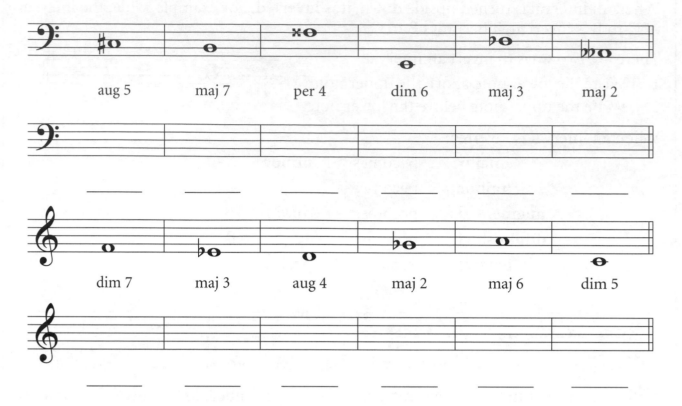

      aug 5        maj 7        per 4        dim 6        maj 3        maj 2

      dim 7        maj 3        aug 4        maj 2        maj 6        dim 5

4. Write the following intervals above the given notes.

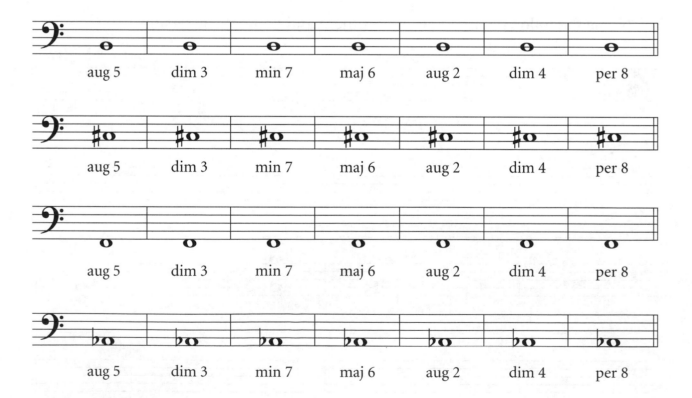

      aug 5     dim 3     min 7     maj 6     aug 2     dim 4     per 8

      aug 5     dim 3     min 7     maj 6     aug 2     dim 4     per 8

      aug 5     dim 3     min 7     maj 6     aug 2     dim 4     per 8

      aug 5     dim 3     min 7     maj 6     aug 2     dim 4     per 8

5. Learn the following Italian terms and their definitions.

| | |
|---|---|
| *accelerando* | becoming quicker |
| *a tempo* | return to the previous tempo |
| *alla* | in the manner of |
| *assai* | much, very much (for example, *allegro assai*: very fast) |
| *ben* | well |
| *col, colla* | with |
| *coll'ottava* | with an added octave |
| *con moto* | with movement |

## Intervals Below a Note

So far, we have written intervals above a given note. Intervals can also be written below a given note.

To write intervals below a given note, follow these three steps:

1. Determine the bottom note of the interval by counting down the required number of notes from the given note.

   In the example below, the given note is G and the requested interval is an augmented 4th. Counting down four notes from G, we get D.

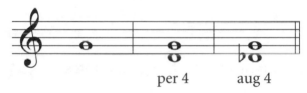

per 4      aug 4

2. Identify the interval using the *bottom* note as the tonic. In the example, D to G is a perfect 4th.

3. Adjust the *bottom* note to obtain the required interval. In the example, D is lowered to D flat to change the interval from a perfect 4th to an augmented 4th.

Here is another example: write a minor 3rd below C sharp.

1. Count down three notes from C sharp (A).

2. Name the resulting interval (major 3rd)

3. Adjust the bottom note to obtain the required interval (change A to A sharp to change the interval from a major 3rd to a minor 3rd).

maj 3      min 3

# INTERVALS

## Checklist

Here is a handy checklist for adjusting intervals:

1. To make a *major* interval *minor*—*raise* the bottom note *one* semitone.

2. To make a *major* interval *diminished*—*raise* the bottom note *two* semitones.

3. To make a *perfect* interval *diminished*—*raise* the bottom note *one* semitone.

4. To make a *major or perfect* interval *augmented*—*lower* the bottom note *one* semitone.

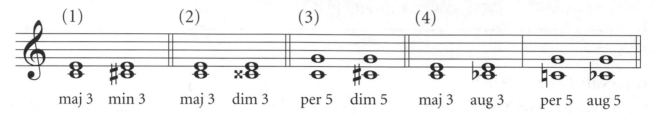

Always identify an interval by using the *lowest* note as the tonic. This applies to melodic intervals, even when the lower note comes after the upper note.

C to F = perfect 4th

1. Write the following intervals below the given notes.

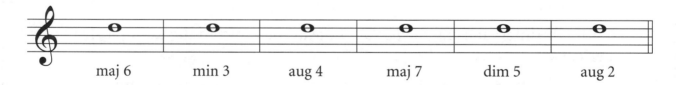

2.  Name the following intervals. Invert them and name the inversion.

3.  Name all of the intervals found between the notes of this melody.

4.  Write three different major 3rds using notes from the scale of D major.

5.  Write four different minor 3rds using notes from the scale of G minor.

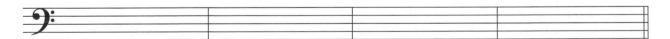

6.  Write four different major 2nds using notes from the scale of E flat major.

# INTERVALS

Occasionally, you may be asked to name one key that includes a number of different intervals. To do this, list all the accidentals—just as if you were trying to determine the key of a melody without a key signature.

In the example below, the accidentals are B flat and C sharp. The key of D minor has a key signature of one flat, and the raised leading note is C sharp.

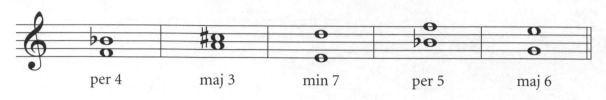

**A**    1.    Name the following intervals. Name one key in which they are all contained.

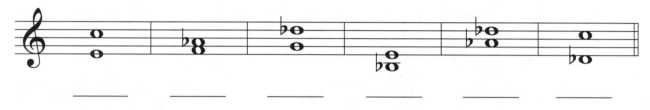

key: _____

key: _____

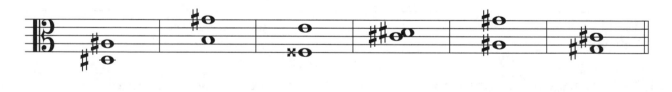

key: _____

## Compound Intervals

An interval that is larger than an octave is called a **compound interval**.

The easiest way to identify a compound interval is to reduce it down to its simple form within the range of an octave. To do this, move the top note down one octave or the bottom note up one octave.

The quality (perfect, major, minor, augmented, or diminished) of the reduced interval is the same as that of the compound interval.

In the first example below, a perfect 12th is reduced to a perfect 5th by moving the top note down an octave. (A perfect 12th is also known as a compound perfect 5th.)

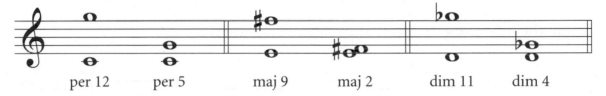

There are three ways to invert a compound interval:

1.  Write the bottom note two octaves higher.
2.  Write the top note two octaves lower.
3.  Write the upper note down one octave and the lower note up one octave.

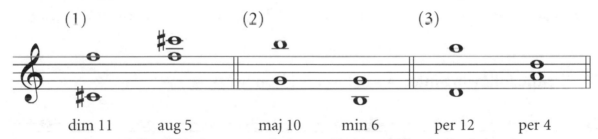

Whichever method you use, make sure that the notes are flipped—the bottom note is on the top or *vice versa*.

The augmented octave is a compound interval since it is larger than a perfect octave. When it is inverted, it becomes a diminished octave.

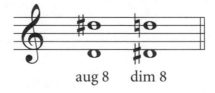

## INTERVALS

 1. Name the following intervals.

2. Write the following intervals above the given notes.

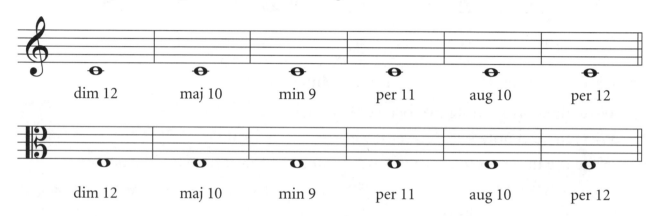

dim 12      maj 10      min 9      per 11      aug 10      per 12

dim 12      maj 10      min 9      per 11      aug 10      per 12

3. Write the following intervals below the given notes.

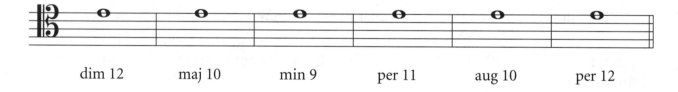

dim 12      maj 10      min 9      per 11      aug 10      per 12

4.  Name the following intervals. Invert them and name the inversions.

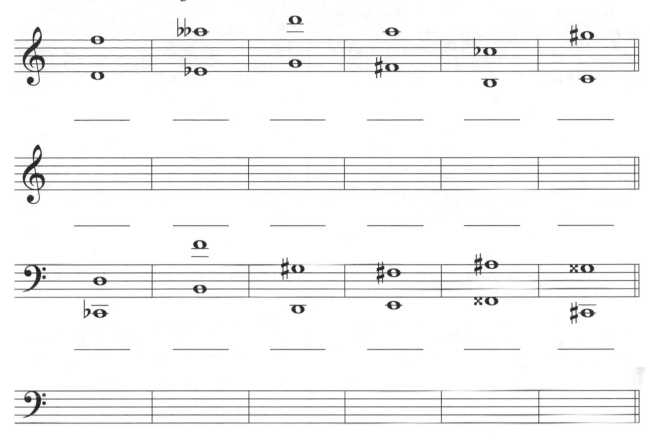

 **Enharmonic Change**

When the name of a note is changed without a change in pitch, it is called an **enharmonic change**. When two note names (for example, C sharp and D flat) refer to the same pitch, they are called **enharmonic equivalents**.

All intervals have enharmonic equivalents. The two intervals sound the same but they have different names. There are three ways to change an interval enharmonically:

1.  Rewrite the upper note without changing its pitch.
2.  Rewrite the lower note without changing its pitch.
3.  Rewrite both notes without changing their pitches.

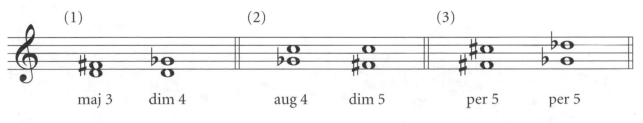

# INTERVALS

1. Name the following intervals. Change the lower note enharmonically and name the new interval.

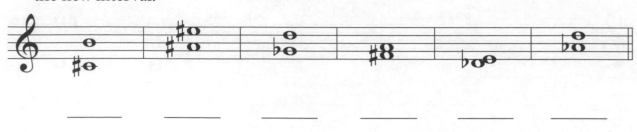

2. Name the following intervals. Change the upper note enharmonically and name the new interval.

3. Name the melodic intervals formed by the notes under the brackets.

Wolfgang Amadeus Mozart
(1756–1791)

Ludwig van Beethoven
(1770–1827)

Edvard Grieg
(1843–1907)

4. Learn the following Italian terms and their definitions.

**A**

| | |
|---|---|
| *ad libitum* | at the liberty of the performer |
| *con fuoco* | with fire |
| *giocoso* | humorous, jocose |
| *pesante* | weighty, with emphasis |
| *risoluto* | resolute |
| *ritenuto* | suddenly slower, held back |
| *scherzando* | playful |
| *sonore* | sonorous |
| *sopra* | above |
| *vivo* | lively |

# SIMPLE TIME

**B** **I** **A**

The staff is divided by **bar lines** into **measures**. A **double bar** at the end of a staff indicates the end of a piece of music.

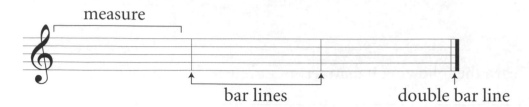

measure

bar lines          double bar line

Beats are grouped together in measures. A measure may contain two, three, four or more beats.

Two numbers are placed at the beginning of a piece of music. The top number indicates the number of beats in each measure. The bottom number tells us which note gets the beat. These numbers are called the **time signature**.

In **simple duple time**, the upper number of the time signature is always **2.** This means that there are two beats in each measure. The lower number, which indicates the note that receives one beat, can be 2, 4, 8, or 16.

$\begin{matrix} \mathbf{2} \\ \mathbf{2} \end{matrix}$   two beats in each measure
the half note receives one beat

¢ is a symbol for $\begin{matrix} \mathbf{2} \\ \mathbf{2} \end{matrix}$ time, also called **cut time** or *alla breve*.

$\begin{matrix} \mathbf{2} \\ \mathbf{4} \end{matrix}$   two beats in each measure
the quarter note receives one beat

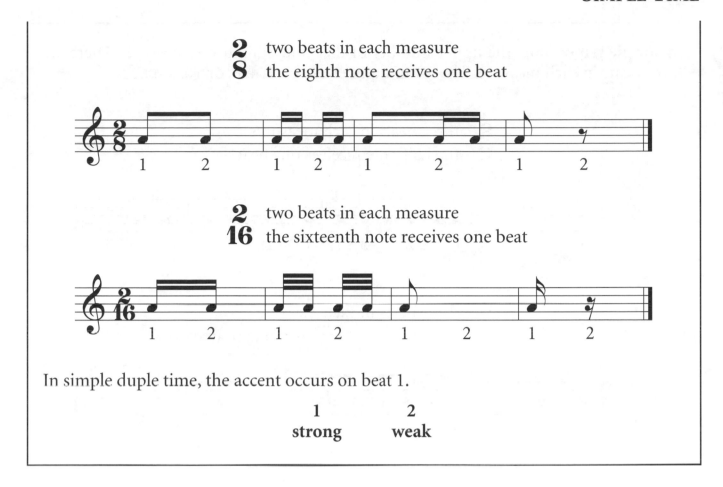

In simple duple time, the accent occurs on beat 1.

| 1 | 2 |
|---|---|
| strong | weak |

1. Add bar lines. Write the beats below each measure.

In **simple triple time**, the upper number of the time signature is always **3**. There are three beats in each measure. The lower number can be 2, 4, 8, or 16.

**3**
**2** three beats in each measure
the half note receives one beat

**3**
**4** three beats in each measure
the quarter note receives one beat

**3**
**8** three beats in each measure
the eighth note receives one beat

**3**
**16** three beats in each measure
the sixteenth note receives one beat

In simple triple time, the accent occurs on beat 1.

| **1** | **2** | **3** |
|---|---|---|
| **strong** | **weak** | **weak** |

**B**
**I**
**A**

2. Add bar lines. Write the beats below each measure.

In **simple quadruple time**, the upper number of the time signature is always **4**. There are four beats in each measure. The lower number can be 2, 4, 8, or 16.

$\dfrac{4}{2}$ four beats in each measure
the half note receives one beat

In $\dfrac{4}{2}$ time, the **double whole note** and **double whole rest,** also called a **breve** and **breve rest**, are equal to four beats (four half notes).

$\dfrac{4}{4}$ four beats in each measure
the quarter note receives one beat

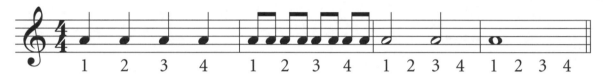

𝄴 is a symbol for $\dfrac{4}{4}$ time, which is also called **common time.**

$\dfrac{4}{8}$ four beats in each measure
the eighth note receives one beat

$\dfrac{4}{16}$ four beats in each measure
the sixteenth note receives one beat

In **simple quadruple time**, the accent occurs on beat 1.

| 1 | 2 | 3 | 4 |
|---|---|---|---|
| strong | weak | medium | weak |

3.   Add bar lines. Write the beats below each measure.

### Incomplete Measures

Not all music begins on a strong beat. When a piece begins with an incomplete measure, the time is subtracted from the last measure. The note or notes in the incomplete measure are called an *anacrusis* or pickup. The first measure plus the last measure equal one complete bar.

### Triplets

A **triplet** is a group of three notes that are played in the time of two notes of the same value.

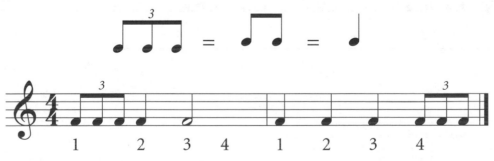

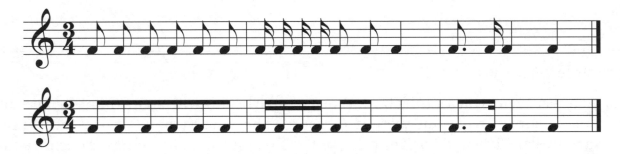

**B I A**

### Grouping Notes

When grouping notes in simple duple time, finish each beat in turn. If the rhythm has notes of the same value, join beats 1 and 2. If the rhythm has notes of different values, do not join beats 1 and 2.

When grouping notes in simple triple time, finish each beat in turn. If the rhythm has notes of the same value, join beats 1 and 2, or beats 1, 2, and 3. If the rhythm has notes of different value, do not join the beats.

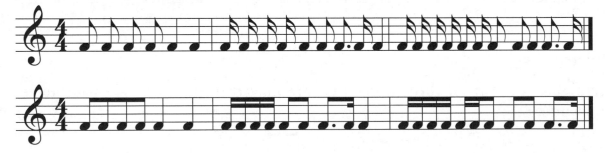

When grouping notes in simple quadruple time, finish each beat in turn. If the rhythm has notes of different value, do not join the beats.

4. Add time signatures to the following melodies.

# Simple Time

5. Add bar lines to the following melodies according to the time signatures.

6. Add time signatures to the following melodies.

## Adding Rests to a Measure in Simple Time

A whole rest may be used to indicate a whole measure of silence in any time signature.

When adding rests to a measure in simple time, place them so that they show one complete beat. Four beats may be combined in a whole rest.

In quadruple time, join beats 1 and 2 or beats 3 and 4 in a single rest, but use separate rests for beats 2 and 3.

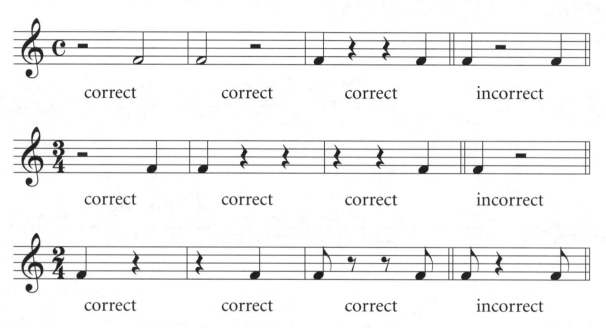

Use rests of less than one beat to finish an incomplete beat. Be sure to finish an incomplete beat before beginning the next one.

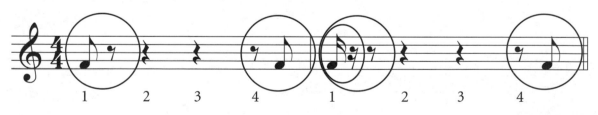

When writing rests in **simple duple time**, finish beat 1 before adding rests for beat 2.

When writing rests in **simple triple time**, finish an incomplete beat before adding the next beat. Join beats 1 and 2 (a strong beat and weak beat) into a single rest, but do not join beats 2 and 3 (a weak beat and weak beat).

When writing rests in **simple quadruple time**, finish an incomplete beat before beginning the next beat. Join beats 1 and 2 (a strong beat and weak beat) into a single rest, but do not join beats 2 and 3 (a weak beat and medium beat).

1. Add rests under the brackets according to the time signatures.

## SIMPLE TIME

*THE COMPLETE ELEMENTARY MUSIC RUDIMENTS*

2. Add time signatures to the following rhythms.

# SIMPLE TIME

3. Add rests under the brackets according to the time signatures.

*THE COMPLETE ELEMENTARY MUSIC RUDIMENTS*

**I**
**A**

### More on Triplets

A **triplet** is a group of *three* notes that are played in the time of *two* notes of the same value. They are most frequently found in simple time.

Triplets are usually indicated by a "*3*"—for example:

Here are some examples of the different ways triplets can be used:

(a)  *Three* eighth notes played in the time of *two* eighth notes equal one beat.

(b)  *Three* sixteenth notes played in the time of *two* sixteenth notes equal one half beat.

(c)  This triplet has only two notes. Together, the quarter and the eighth notes are equal to *three* eighth notes, but they are played in the time of *two* eighth notes.

(d)  This triplet has a dotted rhythm. Once again, the three-note rhythm is equal to *three* eighth notes that are played in the time of *two* eighth notes.

# SIMPLE TIME

1. Add bar lines to the following rhythms according to the time signatures.

2. Add time signatures to the following rhythms.

*THE COMPLETE ELEMENTARY MUSIC RUDIMENTS*

# COMPOUND TIME

**I / A**

In **compound time**, the basic beat is a dotted note. Time signatures in compound time have 6 (compound duple), 9 (compound triple), or 12 (compound quadruple) as the upper number.

In **compound duple time**, there are two beats in each measure. A beat is a group of three pulses and is represented by a dotted note. The upper number of the time signature is always 6, which indicates that each measure contains six pulses (two beats of three pulses). The lower number, which indicates the note that receives one pulse, can be 4, 8, or 16.

**6**
**4**  six pulses (two beats) in each measure
     the quarter note receives one pulse

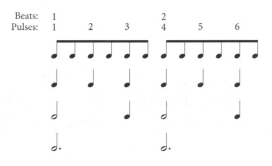

**6**
**8**  six pulses (two beats) in each measure
     the eighth note receives one pulse

**6**
**16** six pulses (two beats) in each measure
     the sixteenth note receives one pulse

# Compound Time

In **compound triple time**, there are three beats in each measure. The upper number of the time signature is always 9, which indicates that each measure contains nine pulses (three beats of three pulses). The lower number, which indicates the note that receives one pulse, can be 4, 8, or 16.

**9**
**4**  nine pulses (three beats) in each measure
the quarter note receives one pulse

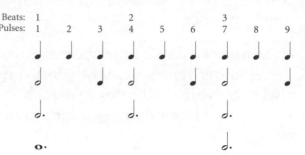

**9**
**8**  nine pulses (three beats) in each measure
the eighth note receives one pulse

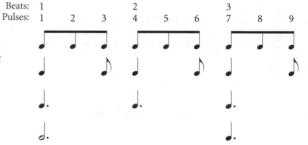

**9**
**16**  nine pulses (three beats) in each measure
the sixteenth note receives one pulse

In **compound quadruple time**, there are four beats in each measure. The upper number of the time signature is always 12, which indicates that each measure contains twelve pulses (four beats of three pulses). The lower number, which indicates the note that receives one pulse, can be 4, 8, or 16.

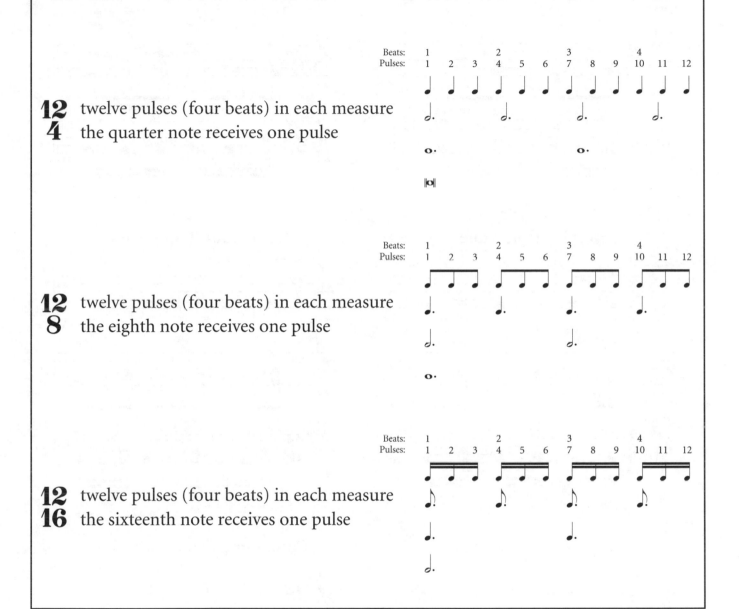

**12**
**4**    twelve pulses (four beats) in each measure
the quarter note receives one pulse

**12**
**8**    twelve pulses (four beats) in each measure
the eighth note receives one pulse

**12**
**16**    twelve pulses (four beats) in each measure
the sixteenth note receives one pulse

In compound time, as in simple time, a whole rest is used to indicate an entire measure of silence in any time signature.

Remember that notes are grouped in three-pulse patterns in compound time. Rests must also follow this three-pulse pattern.

When adding rests to complete the *first two pulses* of a three-pulse group in compound time, *use one rest.*

When adding rests to complete the *last two pulses* of a three-pulse group in compound time, *use two rests.*

In compound triple time, you may *join beats 1 and 2,* but *do not join beats 2 and 3.*

In compound quadruple time, you may complete the *first or last half of the bar with one dotted rest. Do not join beats 2 and 3 into one rest.*

# COMPOUND TIME

**I**

**A**

1. Add rests under the brackets according to the time signatures.

*THE COMPLETE ELEMENTARY MUSIC RUDIMENTS*

2. Add bar lines to the following melodies.

# COMPOUND TIME

The **thirty-second** and **sixty-fourth** notes and rests are written as follows:

**Thirty-second** note and rest        **Sixty-fourth** note and rest

4 thirty-second notes        equal        2 sixteenth notes        equal        1 eighth note

## Double Dotted Notes

When two dots are placed beside a note or rest:

1.  The first dot increases the duration by half the value of the note or rest.
2.  The second dot increases the duration by half the value of the first dot.

3. Add time signatures to the following one-measure rhythms. The rhythms may be in simple or compound time.

# COMPOUND TIME

### Irregular Groups

A **duplet** is a group of *two* notes that are played in the time of *three* notes of the same value. Duplets are found in *compound time*.

A **quadruplet** is a group of *four* notes that are played in the time of *three* notes of the same value. Quadruplets are found in *compound time*.

A **quintuplet** is a group of *five* notes that are played in the time of *three, four, or six* notes of the same value, depending on the time signature.

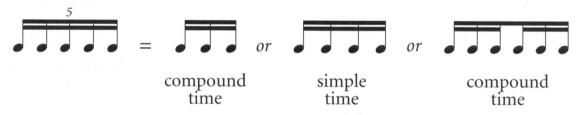

A **sextuplet** is a group of *six* notes that are played in the time of *four* notes of the same value.

A **septuplet** is a group of *seven* notes that are played in the time of *three or four* notes of the same value, depending on the time signature.

To determine the value of an irregular group of notes, examine the remaining beats (and partial beats) in the measure. The irregular group will fill the remaining beats (or partial beats) required to complete the measure.

**I**
**A**
1. Add bar lines to the following melodies according to the time signatures.

Franz Joseph Haydn
(1732–1809)

Franz Joseph Haydn
(1732–1809)

Frédéric Chopin
(1810–1849)

Pyotr Il'yich Tchaikovsky
(1840–1893)

Edvard Grieg
(1843–1907)

Johannes Brahms
(1833–1897)

Robert Schumann
(1810–1856)

Niccolò Paganini
(1782–1840)

## COMPOUND TIME

2. Add rests under the brackets according to the time signatures.

### Syncopation

Syncopation occurs when the pattern of strong and weak beats in a measure is altered, and the accent is shifted from the strong beat to the weak beat.

3. Write three-measure rhythms for the following time signatures. (Use a different rhythm for each measure.)

# COMPOUND TIME

4. Add time signatures to the following one-measure rhythms.

5. Add rests under the brackets according to the time signatures.

## COMPOUND TIME

6. Add stems to the following noteheads and group them to create one-measure rhythms according to the time signatures.

7. Learn the following Italian terms and their definitions.

| | |
|---|---|
| *non* | not |
| *non troppo* | not too much |
| *ottava, 8va* | the interval of an octave |
| *più* | more |
| *più mosso* | more movement (quicker) |
| *poco* | little |
| *poco a poco* | little by little |
| *quasi* | almost, as if |
| *sempre* | always, continuously |

# Hybrid Meters

**H**ybrid meters combine simple and compound time. They can be duple, triple, or quadruple.

**Hybrid Duple Time**

In **hybrid duple time,** each measure contains *five* pulses that are grouped into *two* beats. Usually, the pulses are grouped in a 3 + 2 pattern, but they can also be grouped in a 2 + 3 pattern.

The upper number of the time signature is always 5. The lower number can be 2, 4, 8, or 16.

Notes that are the value of an eighth or less are joined together by a beam if they belong to the same beat. A sound that is held for a complete measure must be written as two notes joined by a tie.

**A** 1. Add bar lines to the following rhythms.

# HYBRID METERS

### Hybrid Triple Time

In **hybrid triple time**, each measure contains *seven* pulses that are grouped into *three* beats. The first beat is the strong beat. The pulses are usually grouped in a 3 + 2 + 2 pattern, but they can also be grouped in a 2 + 3 + 2 or 2 + 2 + 3 pattern.

The upper number of the time signature is always 7. The lower number can be 2, 4, 8, or 16.

Notes that are the value of an eighth or less are joined together by a beam if they belong to the same beat. A sound that is held for a complete measure must be written as three notes joined by a tie.

1.  Add bar lines to the following rhythms.

**Hybrid Quadruple Time**

In **hybrid quadruple time**, the upper number of the time signature may be 9, 10, or 11, and the lower number may be 2, 4, 8, or 16.

There are four beats to the measure, and each beat contains either two or three pulses, as shown in the examples below.

 1. Add bar lines to the following rhythms.

# HYBRID METERS

2. Add time signatures to the following rhythms.

*THE COMPLETE ELEMENTARY MUSIC RUDIMENTS*

3.  Rewrite the following rhythms, grouping the notes according to the time signatures. Add bar lines.

# Hybrid Meters

4. Add bar lines to the following excerpts according to the time signatures.

Ludwig van Beethoven
(1770–1827)

Frédéric Chopin
(1810–1849)

Pyotr Il'yich Tchaikovsky
(1840–1893)

### Rests in Hybrid Time

Here are some important points about writing rests in hybrid time:

1. Use a whole rest to indicate a complete measure of rest.

2. In hybrid duple time, there are two beats to the measure with an accent pattern of *strong–weak*. Complete each beat with a single rest.

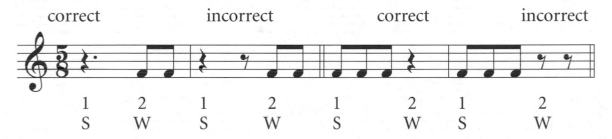

3. In hybrid triple time, there are three beats to the measure with an accent pattern of *strong–weak–weak*. You may combine a strong beat followed by a weak beat into a single rest, but do not combine two weak beats into one rest.

4. In hybrid quadruple time, there are four beats to the measure with an accent pattern of *strong–weak–medium–weak*. You may combine a strong beat followed by a weak beat or a medium beat followed by a weak beat into a single rest. Do not combine a weak beat followed by a medium beat into one rest. Also, do not combine a compound beat (a group of three pulses) and a simple beat (a group of two pulses) into one rest.

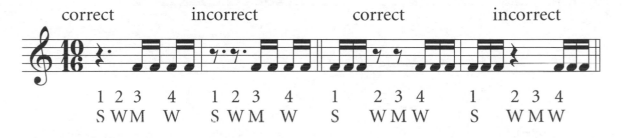

## Hybrid Meters

**A** 1. Add rests under the brackets to complete the following measures.

*The Complete Elementary Music Rudiments*

2. Add bar lines to the following melodies according to the time signatures.

# HYBRID METERS

3.  Add time signatures to the following one-measure rhythms.

4.   Add rests under the brackets to complete the following measures.

# CHORDS

A **chord** is a combination of notes that are played together.

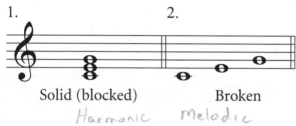

A **triad** is a three-note chord.

Triads can be written and played in two ways:
1. **Solid (blocked)**—all three notes are written, or sound, at the same time.
2. **Broken**—each note is written, or is played, one after the other.

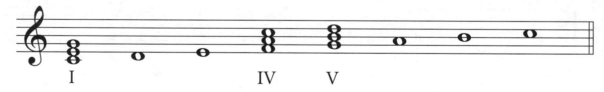

The lowest note of a triad is called the **root.** The next note is called the **third,** because it is the interval of a 3rd above the root of the triad. The final note is called the **fifth,** because it is the interval of a 5th above the root.

Triads may be built on any of the seven degrees of a major or minor scale.

These are triads built on the tonic, subdominant, and dominant degrees of the C major scale:

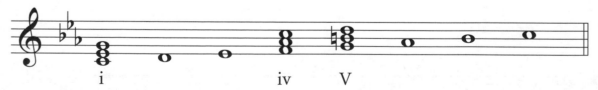

These are triads built on the tonic, subdominant, and dominant degrees of the C minor scale:

Notice that the dominant triads in tonic major and minor keys (for example, C major and C minor above) are the same. *The third of the dominant triad in a minor key is the leading note (seventh), and must be raised.*

A **major triad** consists of the intervals of a major 3rd and a perfect 5th above the root.

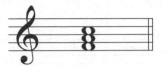

F to A = maj 3    F to C = per 5

A **minor triad** consists of the intervals of a minor 3rd and a perfect 5th above the root.

F to A♭ = min 3    F to C = per 5

**B**
**I**
**A**

1. Name the root, third, and fifth of the following triads.

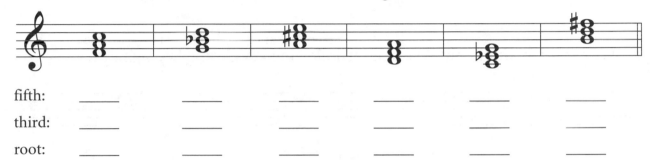

fifth: _____    _____    _____    _____    _____    _____

third: _____    _____    _____    _____    _____    _____

root: _____    _____    _____    _____    _____    _____

2. Identify the following triads as either major or minor.

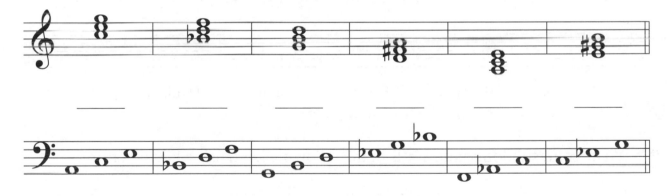

3. Rewrite the following major triads to make them minor triads.

4. Rewrite the following minor triads to make them major triads.

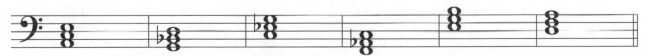

# CHORDS

5. Write solid tonic triads in the following keys, using key signatures.

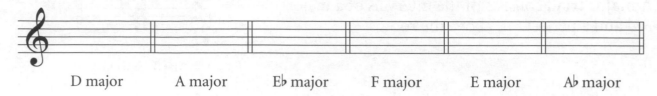

     D major        A major        E♭ major       F major        E major       A♭ major

6. Write broken tonic triads in the following keys, using key signatures.

     E minor        F minor        D minor       C minor       F♯ minor      C♯ minor

7. Write broken dominant triads in the following keys, using key signatures.

     C major       B♭ major      G major       A major      E♭ major      D major

8. Write solid dominant triads in the following keys, using key signatures.

     A minor       G minor       B minor       C minor       D minor      F♯ minor

9. Write solid subdominant triads in the following keys, using key signatures.

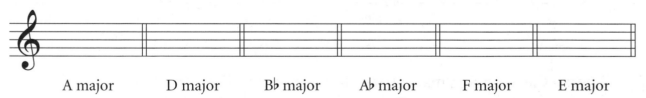

     A major       D major       B♭ major      A♭ major      F major       E major

10. Write broken subdominant triads in the following keys, using key signatures.

     E minor       A minor       F minor      C♯ minor      G minor       D minor

11. For each of the following triads, name the key and the degree on which the triad is built: Tonic (I), Subdominant (IV), or Dominant (V).

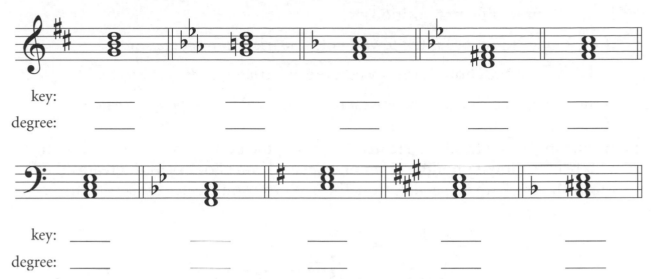

key: \_\_\_\_\_  \_\_\_\_\_  \_\_\_\_\_  \_\_\_\_\_  \_\_\_\_\_

degree: \_\_\_\_\_  \_\_\_\_\_  \_\_\_\_\_  \_\_\_\_\_  \_\_\_\_\_

key: \_\_\_\_\_  \_\_\_\_\_  \_\_\_\_\_  \_\_\_\_\_  \_\_\_\_\_

degree: \_\_\_\_\_  \_\_\_\_\_  \_\_\_\_\_  \_\_\_\_\_  \_\_\_\_\_

12. Write the following broken triads, using accidentals instead of a key signature.

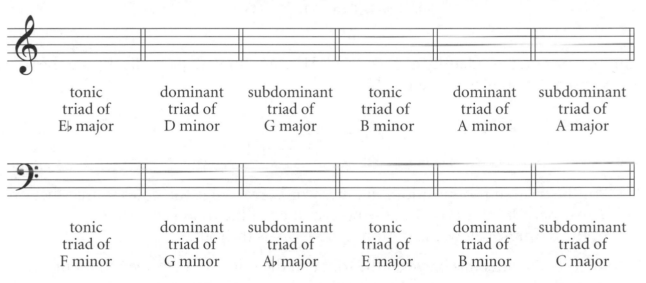

| tonic triad of Eb major | dominant triad of D minor | subdominant triad of G major | tonic triad of B minor | dominant triad of A minor | subdominant triad of A major |

| tonic triad of F minor | dominant triad of G minor | subdominant triad of Ab major | tonic triad of E major | dominant triad of B minor | subdominant triad of C major |

13. Learn the following Italian terms and their definitions.

| *tempo* | speed at which the music is performed |
|---|---|
| *a tempo* | return to the previous tempo |
| *Tempo primo, Tempo I* | return to the original tempo |
| *rallentando, rall.* | slowing down |
| *ritardando, rit.* | slowing down gradually |
| *forte, f* | loud |
| *fortissimo, ff* | very loud |
| *mezzo forte, mf* | moderately loud |
| *mezzo piano, mp* | moderately soft |
| *piano, p* | soft |
| *pianissimo, pp* | very soft |

# CHORDS

## Inversions

Triads can occur in different positions:

1.  If the *root* of the chord is the lowest note, the triad is in *root position.*

2.  If the *third* of the chord is the lowest note, the triad is in *first inversion.*

3.  If the *fifth* of the chord is the lowest note, the triad is in *second inversion.*

The inversions of the triad are created by raising the bottom note one octave. In the example below, moving middle C up one octave from root position creates the first inversion. Moving E up one octave from the first inversion creates the second inversion.

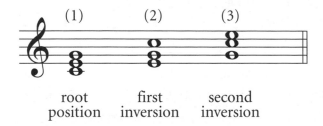

You may be asked to identify a given triad. Here are three steps to determine the root, the type, and the position of a triad:

1.  Put the triad in root position. In other words, rearrange the notes so that they are a 3rd apart. In root position, the bottom note of the triad is the root.
    In the example below, the bottom note—D—is the root.

2.  Identify the intervals between the root and the third, and between the root and the fifth. This will tell you the type of triad (major or minor).

    In the example below, the triad consists of a major 3rd and a perfect 5th. Therefore, it is a major triad.

3.  Look at the lowest note of the given triad. If this note is the root, the triad is in root position. If it is the 3rd, the triad is in first inversion. If it is the 5th, the triad is in second inversion.

    In the given triad, the lowest note—F sharp— is the third of the triad. Therefore, this triad is in first inversion.

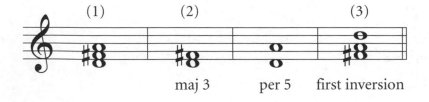

**I**
**A**

1. Write major triads in root position above the given notes. In the measures that follow, write the triads in first and second inversion.

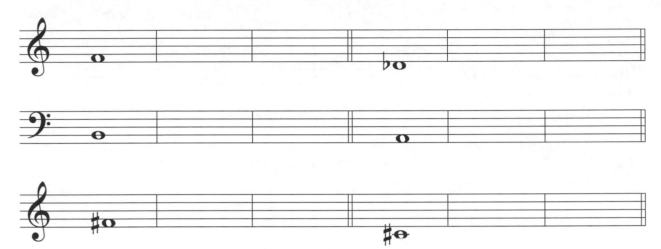

2. Write minor triads in root position above the given notes. In the measures that follow, write the triads in first and second inversion.

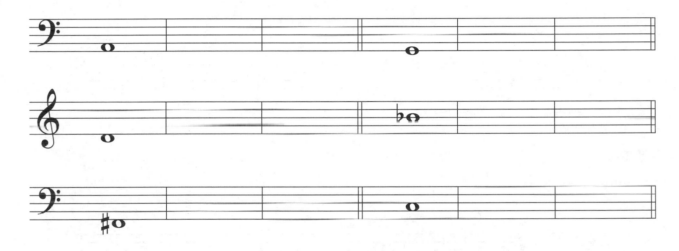

3. Name the roots of the following triads.

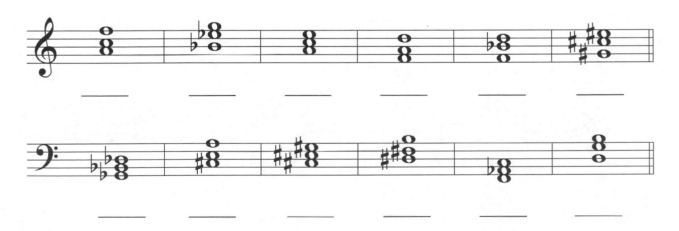

## CHORDS

4. Using key signatures, write root position tonic, subdominant, and dominant triads in the following keys.

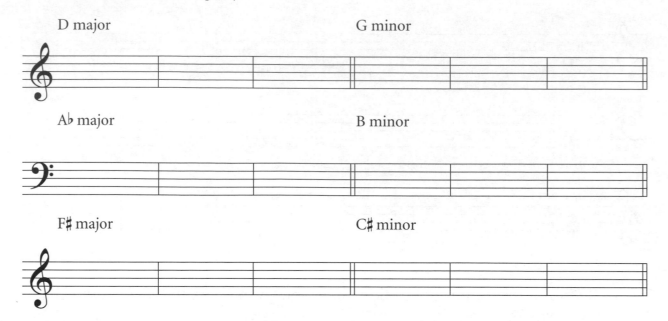

D major          G minor

A♭ major          B minor

F♯ major          C♯ minor

5. Name the root, type, and position of the following triads.

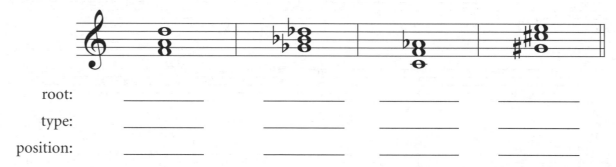

root:   _____   _____   _____   _____

type:   _____   _____   _____   _____

position:   _____   _____   _____   _____

root:   _____   _____   _____   _____

type:   _____   _____   _____   _____

position:   _____   _____   _____   _____

root:   _____   _____   _____   _____

type:   _____   _____   _____   _____

position:   _____   _____   _____   _____

6. Write the following triads in first inversion, using key signatures.

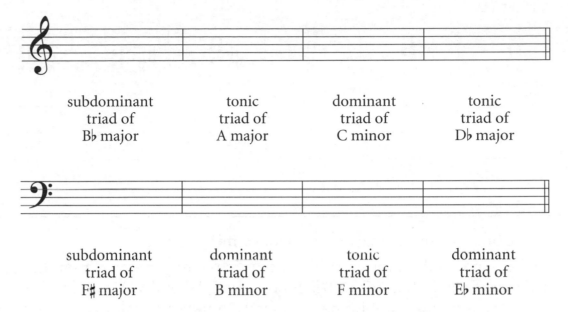

subdominant
triad of
B♭ major

tonic
triad of
A major

dominant
triad of
C minor

tonic
triad of
D♭ major

subdominant
triad of
F♯ major

dominant
triad of
B minor

tonic
triad of
F minor

dominant
triad of
E♭ minor

7. Write the following triads in root position, using accidentals instead of a key signature.

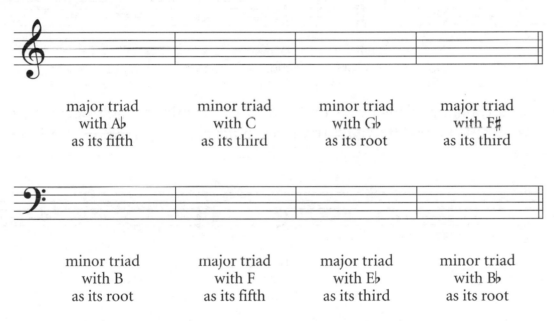

major triad
with A♭
as its fifth

minor triad
with C
as its third

minor triad
with G♭
as its root

major triad
with F♯
as its third

minor triad
with B
as its root

major triad
with F
as its fifth

major triad
with E♭
as its third

minor triad
with B♭
as its root

8. Write the following triads, using accidentals instead of a key signature.

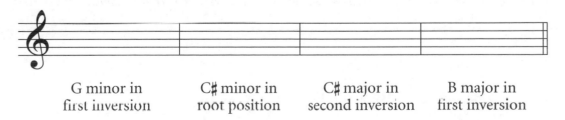

G minor in
first inversion

C♯ minor in
root position

C♯ major in
second inversion

B major in
first inversion

# CHORDS

9. Name the root, type, and position of the following triads.

root: _____ _____ _____ _____ _____ _____

type: _____ _____ _____ _____ _____ _____

position: _____ _____ _____ _____ _____ _____

Triads can be built on any degree of the major or minor scale.

These are the major and minor triads that occur in the major scale. From the example below in C major, we see that major triads occur on I, IV, and V. Minor triads occur on ii, iii, and vi. We use uppercase Roman numerals to indicate scale degrees with major triads and lowercase numerals to indicate scale degrees with minor triads.

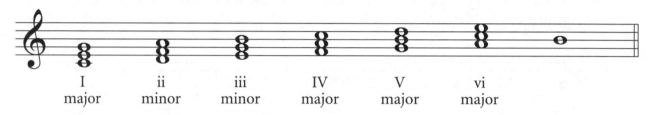

|  I  |  ii  |  iii  |  IV  |  V  |  vi  |
| major | minor | minor | major | major | major |

In a minor key, major triads occur on V and VI, and minor triads occur on i and iv. Study the example below, in which triads are built on the degrees of the A harmonic minor scale.

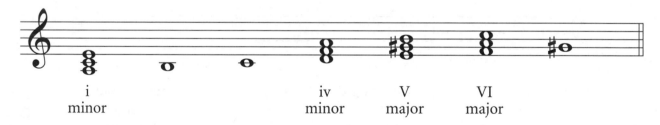

|  i  |  |  |  iv  |  V  |  VI  |
| minor |  |  | minor | major | major |

Triads take the same name as the scale degrees they are built upon. For example, a triad built on the third note of the C major scale is called the *mediant triad of C major*. A triad built on the fifth note of the A minor scale is called the *dominant triad of A minor*.

1. Name the root, type, and position of the following chords. Then name the major key in which each triad can be found and name the scale degree on which each is built.

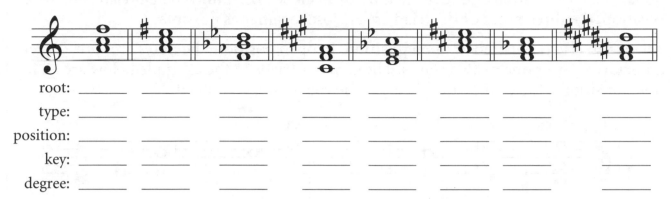

root: \_\_\_\_\_ \_\_\_\_\_ \_\_\_\_\_ \_\_\_\_\_ \_\_\_\_\_ \_\_\_\_\_ \_\_\_\_\_ \_\_\_\_\_

type: \_\_\_\_\_ \_\_\_\_\_ \_\_\_\_\_ \_\_\_\_\_ \_\_\_\_\_ \_\_\_\_\_ \_\_\_\_\_ \_\_\_\_\_

position: \_\_\_\_\_ \_\_\_\_\_ \_\_\_\_\_ \_\_\_\_\_ \_\_\_\_\_ \_\_\_\_\_ \_\_\_\_\_ \_\_\_\_\_

key: \_\_\_\_\_ \_\_\_\_\_ \_\_\_\_\_ \_\_\_\_\_ \_\_\_\_\_ \_\_\_\_\_ \_\_\_\_\_ \_\_\_\_\_

degree: \_\_\_\_\_ \_\_\_\_\_ \_\_\_\_\_ \_\_\_\_\_ \_\_\_\_\_ \_\_\_\_\_ \_\_\_\_\_ \_\_\_\_\_

2. Name the root, type, and position of the following chords. Then name the minor key in which each triad can be found and name the scale degree on which each is built.

root: \_\_\_\_\_ \_\_\_\_\_ \_\_\_\_\_ \_\_\_\_\_ \_\_\_\_\_ \_\_\_\_\_ \_\_\_\_\_ \_\_\_\_\_

type: \_\_\_\_\_ \_\_\_\_\_ \_\_\_\_\_ \_\_\_\_\_ \_\_\_\_\_ \_\_\_\_\_ \_\_\_\_\_ \_\_\_\_\_

position: \_\_\_\_\_ \_\_\_\_\_ \_\_\_\_\_ \_\_\_\_\_ \_\_\_\_\_ \_\_\_\_\_ \_\_\_\_\_ \_\_\_\_\_

key: \_\_\_\_\_ \_\_\_\_\_ \_\_\_\_\_ \_\_\_\_\_ \_\_\_\_\_ \_\_\_\_\_ \_\_\_\_\_ \_\_\_\_\_

degree: \_\_\_\_\_ \_\_\_\_\_ \_\_\_\_\_ \_\_\_\_\_ \_\_\_\_\_ \_\_\_\_\_ \_\_\_\_\_ \_\_\_\_\_

3. Write the following triads, using a key signature for each.

| supertonic | dominant | submediant | subdominant |
| triad of G major | triad of C minor | triad of B♭ major | triad of F minor |
| in first inversion | in root position | in second inversion | in first inversion |

4. Write the following triads, using accidentals instead of a key signature.

| tonic | submediant | mediant | dominant |
| triad of A major | triad of D minor | triad of F major | triad of G minor |
| in second inversion | in root position | in second inversion | in first inversion |

# CHORDS

## Close and Open Position

So far, we have written and identified triads in **close position.** When a triad is in close position, the three notes of the triad are as close together as possible.

Triads can also be written in **open position.** In open position, the notes are spread over an octave or over one or two staves. The C major triads in the example below are all in open position. One of the notes (usually the root) can be doubled.

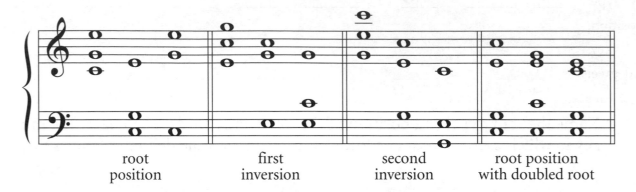

root         first         second        root position
position      inversion     inversion    with doubled root

Remember that the lowest note determines the inversion of the triad.

1.  If the root is the lowest note, the triad is in root position.
2.  If the third is the lowest note, the triad is in first inversion.
3.  If the fifth is the lowest note, the triad is in second inversion.

1.  Name the root, type, and position of the following chords.

root: ____  ____  ____  ____  ____  ____  ____  ____

type: ____  ____  ____  ____  ____  ____  ____  ____

position: ____  ____  ____  ____  ____  ____  ____  ____

2.  Name the root, type, and position of the following chords. Then name the major key in which each triad can be found and name the scale degree on which each is built.

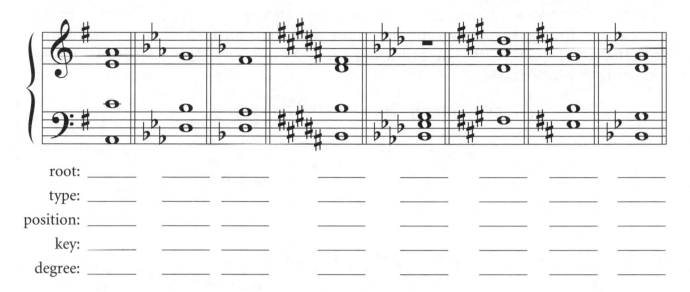

root: _____ _____ _____ _____ _____ _____ _____ _____

type: _____ _____ _____ _____ _____ _____ _____ _____

position: _____ _____ _____ _____ _____ _____ _____ _____

key: _____ _____ _____ _____ _____ _____ _____ _____

degree: _____ _____ _____ _____ _____ _____ _____ _____

3.  Name the root, type, and position of the following chords. Then name the minor key in which each triad can be found and name the scale degree on which each is built.

root: _____ _____ _____ _____ _____ _____ _____ _____

type: _____ _____ _____ _____ _____ _____ _____ _____

position: _____ _____ _____ _____ _____ _____ _____ _____

key: _____ _____ _____ _____ _____ _____ _____ _____

degree: _____ _____ _____ _____ _____ _____ _____ _____

# CHORDS

**Broken Chords in Instrumental Music**

The chords we have studied appear frequently in instrumental music. Sometimes they appear in solid (blocked) form, and sometimes they appear in a variety of broken forms. Study the following pieces and the harmonic reduction of the broken chords in the left-hand accompaniment. The following sonatina has a left-hand accompaniment consisting of broken triads.

### Sonatina, op. 36, no. 1 (2nd movement)

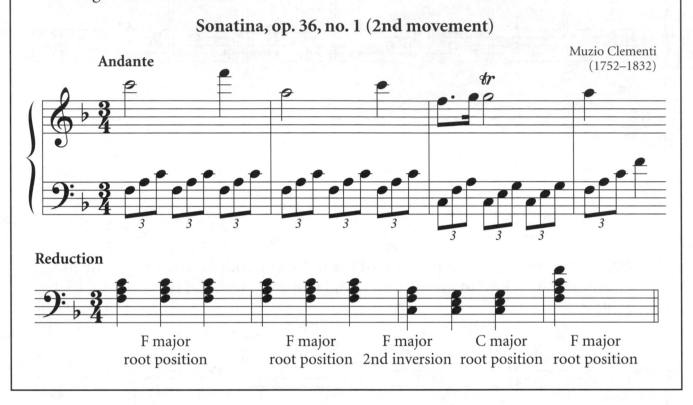

The Kuhlau sonatina below contains a broken-chord pattern in the left hand called an *Alberti bass*. This is a typical accompaniment pattern from the Classical era. The chord in measure 4, a dominant 7th, will be covered in the next lesson.

**Sonatina, op. 20, no. 1 (2nd movement)**

Fredrich Kuhlau
(1786–1832)

**Reduction**

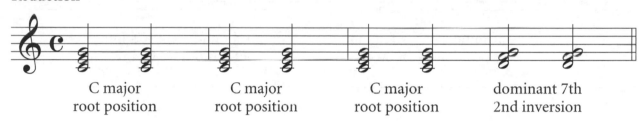

| C major<br>root position | C major<br>root position | C major<br>root position | dominant 7th<br>2nd inversion |

The left-hand accompaniment of the Brahms waltz below uses another broken-chord pattern. This is a common accompaniment for a waltz.

**Waltz, op. 39, no. 3**

Johannes Brahms
(1833–1897)

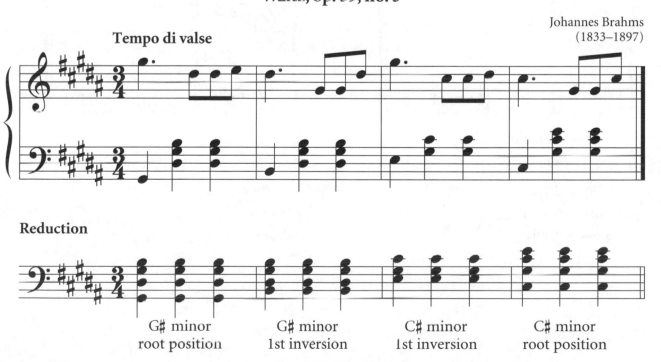

**Tempo di valse**

**Reduction**

| G♯ minor<br>root position | G♯ minor<br>1st inversion | C♯ minor<br>1st inversion | C♯ minor<br>root position |

# CHORDS

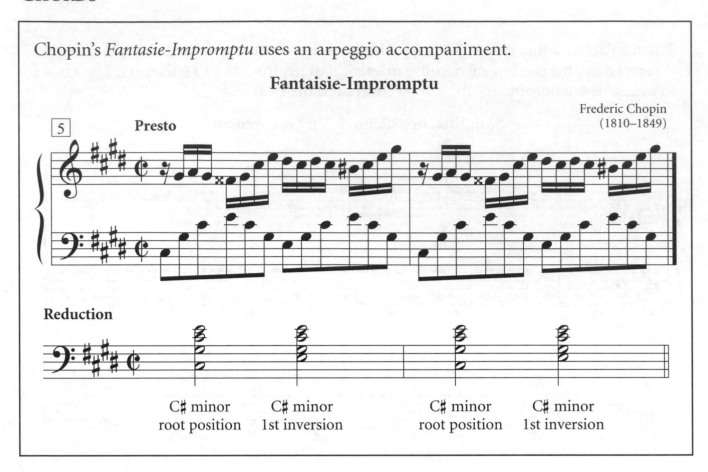

Chopin's *Fantasie-Impromptu* uses an arpeggio accompaniment.

## Fantaisie-Impromptu

Frederic Chopin
(1810–1849)

**Presto**

**Reduction**

C# minor
root position

C# minor
1st inversion

C# minor
root position

C# minor
1st inversion

1. Name the major key of the following musical fragments. State the root, type, position, and scale degree of the triads found in each.

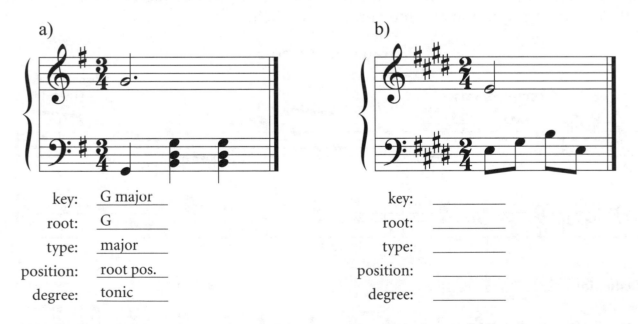

a)

| key: | G major |
|------|---------|
| root: | G |
| type: | major |
| position: | root pos. |
| degree: | tonic |

b)

| key: | ___ |
|------|---------|
| root: | ___ |
| type: | ___ |
| position: | ___ |
| degree: | ___ |

c)

key: _____

root: _____

type: _____

position: _____

degree: _____

d)

key: _____

root: _____

type: _____

position: _____

degree: _____

e)

key: _____

root: _____

type: _____

position: _____

degree: _____

f)

key: _____

root: _____

type: _____

position: _____

degree: _____

2. Name the minor key of the following musical fragments. State the root, type, position, and scale degree of the triads found in each.

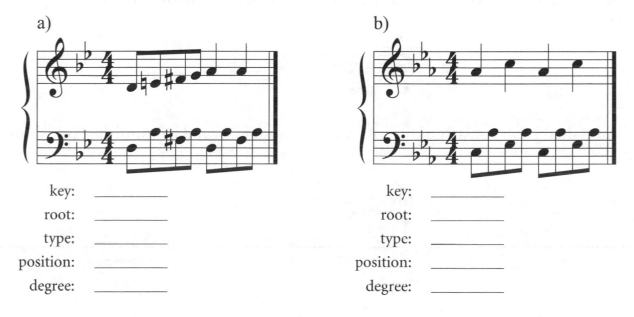

a)

key: _____

root: _____

type: _____

position: _____

degree: _____

b)

key: _____

root: _____

type: _____

position: _____

degree: _____

# CHORDS

c)

key: _____

root: _____

type: _____

position: _____

degree: _____

d)

key: _____

root: _____

type: _____

position: _____

degree: _____

e)

key: _____

root: _____

type: _____

position: _____

degree: _____

f)

key: _____

root: _____

type: _____

position: _____

degree: _____

**A**

An **augmented triad** consists of the intervals of a major 3rd and an augmented 5th above the root.

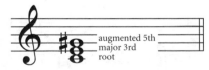

A **diminished triad** consists of the intervals of a minor 3rd and a diminished 5th above the root.

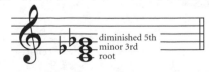

1. Identify the following triads as major, minor, augmented, or diminished.

2. Learn the following Italian terms and their definitions.

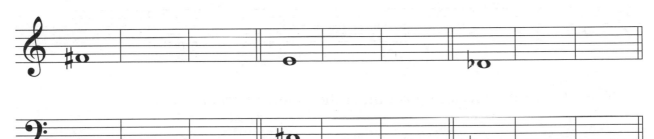

| | |
|---|---|
| *rubato* | a flexible tempo, using slight variations of speed to enhance musical expression |
| *senza* | without |
| *tenuto* | held, sustained |
| *troppo* | too much |
| *una corda* | one string, depress the left (piano) pedal |
| *vivace* | lively, brisk |

3. Write major triads in root position above the given notes. In the measures that follow, write the triads in first and second inversion.

# CHORDS

4. Write minor triads in root position above the given notes. In the measures that follow, write the triads in first and second inversion.

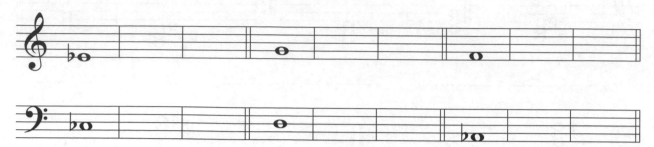

**A** 5. Write diminished triads in root position above the given notes. In the measures that follow, write the triads in first and second inversion.

6. Write augmented triads in root position above the given notes. In the measures that follow, write the triads in first and second inversion.

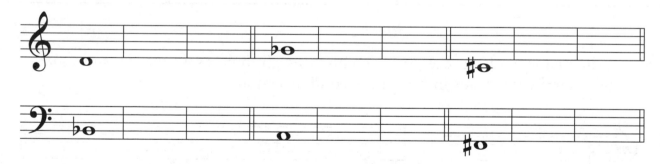

7. Name the root, type, and position of the following triads.

root: _____  _____  _____  _____  _____  _____  _____  _____

type: _____  _____  _____  _____  _____  _____  _____  _____

position: _____  _____  _____  _____  _____  _____  _____  _____

8. Write the following triads:

(a) major triad with G as the root
(b) augmented triad with F♯ as the fifth
(c) minor triad with D♭ as the root
(d) diminished triad with C as the third

(e) minor triad with B as the fifth
(f) diminished triad with E♭ as the third
(g) augmented triad with B as the root
(h) augmented triad with A as the third

**A** 9. Name the root, type, and position of the following triads.

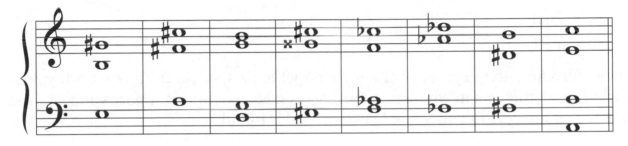

root: ____ ____ ____ ____ ____ ____ ____ ____

type: ____ ____ ____ ____ ____ ____ ____ ____

position: ____ ____ ____ ____ ____ ____ ____ ____

**A**

Triads can be written on any note of the major or minor scale.

In the *major* scale, major triads occur on the tonic, subdominant and dominant. Minor triads occur on the supertonic, mediant and submediant. A diminished triad occurs on the leading note.

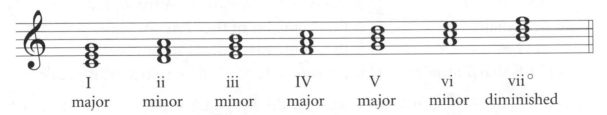

|  I  |  ii  |  iii  |  IV  |  V  |  vi  |  vii°  |
| major | minor | minor | major | major | minor | diminished |

In the *minor* scale, major triads occur on the dominant and submediant. Minor triads occur on the supertonic and subdominant. Diminished triads occur on the supertonic and leading note, and an augmented triad occurs on the mediant.

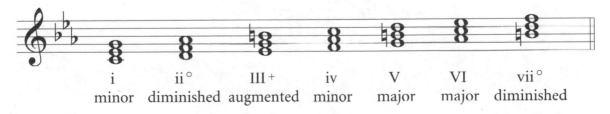

|  i  |  ii°  |  III⁺  |  iv  |  V  |  VI  |  vii°  |
| minor | diminished | augmented | minor | major | major | diminished |

## CHORDS

Triads take the same name as the scale degrees they are built upon.

Triads and chords are identified with Roman numerals. Major and augmented triads use capital or uppercase Roman numerals, and minor and diminished triads use lowercase Roman numerals. A small degree sign (○) placed after a lowercase Roman numeral indicates a diminished triad and a plus sign (+) after an uppercase Roman numeral indicates an augmented triad.

Here is a summary of the triads built on different scale degrees:

| Type of Triad | Major Scales | Minor Scales |
|---|---|---|
| major | I, IV, V | V, VI |
| minor | ii, iii, vi | i, iv |
| diminished | vii° | ii°, vii° |
| augmented | | III+ |

Since you know the degrees of the scale on which a specific triad is found, you can determine all the keys in which that triad occurs. For example, suppose you were asked to name all the keys in which the D major triad is found.

1.  Name the degrees of the major and minor scales on which major triads are built. Major triads are found on the tonic, subdominant, and dominant of the major scale, and on dominant and submediant of the minor scale.

2.  Match the scale degrees with their appropriate keys.
    The D major triad is:

| | |
|---|---|
| I of D major | – D is the *tonic* of the D major scale |
| IV of A major | – D is the *subdominant* of the A major scale |
| V of G major | – D is the *dominant* of the G major scale |
| V of G minor | – D is the *dominant* of the G minor scale |
| VI of F sharp minor | – D is the *submediant* of the F sharp minor scale |

Therefore, the D major triad occurs in the keys of D major, A major, G major, G minor, and F sharp minor.

Here is another example. Name the keys in which the E diminished triad occurs.

1. A diminished triad is found on the leading note of the major scale, and on the supertonic and leading note of the minor scale.

2. The E diminished triad is:

    vii° of F major   –   E is the *leading note* of the F major scale
    II° of D minor   –   E is the *supertonic* of the D minor scale
    VII° of F minor   –   E is the *leading note* of the F minor scale

    The E diminished triad occurs in the keys of F major, D minor, and F minor.

1. Write all the triads in the key of D major. Identify the type of each one.

degree:    I      ii      iii      IV      V      vi      vii°

type: _____ _____ _____ _____ _____ _____ _____

2. Write all the triads in the key of A♭ major. Identify the scale degree and the type of each one.

degree:

type: _____ _____ _____ _____ _____ _____ _____

3. Write all the triads in the key of C♯ minor. Identify the scale degree and the type of each one.

degree:

type: _____ _____ _____ _____ _____ _____ _____

4. Write all the triads in the key of G minor. Identify the scale degree and the type of each one.

degree:

type: _____ _____ _____ _____ _____ _____ _____

*THE COMPLETE ELEMENTARY MUSIC RUDIMENTS*    173

# CHORDS

5. Name all the keys in which the following triads may be found.

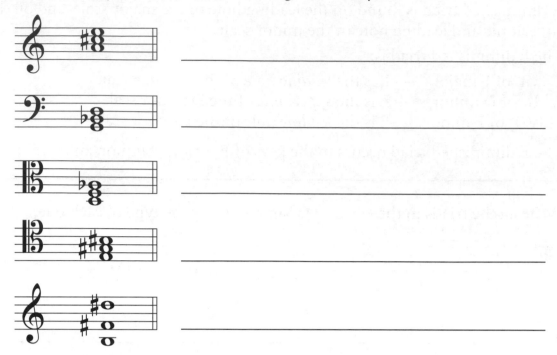

_____

_____

_____

_____

_____

6. Write the one triad that is found in C major, A minor, and C minor.

7. Write the one triad that is found only in A minor.

8. Write the following triads:

(a) diminished triad found in the key of F major
(b) augmented triad found in the key of B♭ minor
(c) diminished triad found in the key of F♯ major
(d) augmented triad found in the key of E minor
(e) diminished triad found in the key of A major
(f) augmented triad found in the key of F minor
(g) diminished triad found in the key of D♭ major
(h) augmented triad found in the key of C♯ minor

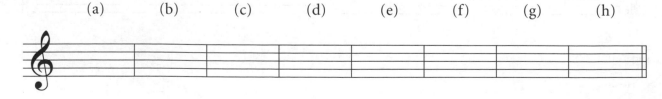

| (a) | (b) | (c) | (d) | (e) | (f) | (g) | (h) |

9.  Using key signatures, write dominant triads in the following keys.

    Eb major          C# minor          F minor          B major          Ab minor

10. Using key signatures, write supertonic triads in the following keys.

    Bb major          A minor          G major          B minor          F# major

11. Using key signatures, write leading-note triads in the following keys.

    E major          G minor          F major          D# minor          Bb minor

12. Learn the following French terms and their definitions.

**A**

| *cédez* | yield; hold back the tempo |
| *lentement* | slowly |
| *modéré* | at a moderate tempo |
| *vite* | fast |
| *léger* | light, lightly |
| *mouvement* | tempo, motion |

# THE DOMINANT 7TH CHORD

**A**

The **dominant 7th chord** is a four-note chord that consists of a *dominant triad* plus a *minor 7th* above the root. In other words, the intervals above the root of a dominant 7th chord are a major 3rd, a perfect 5th, and a minor 7th. The symbol for a dominant 7th chord is V⁷.

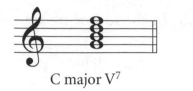
C major V⁷

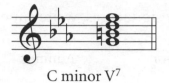
C minor V⁷

Tonic major and minor keys have the same dominant 7th. The key of a dominant 7th chord is a perfect 5th below the root of the chord. For example, the dominant 7th chord with A as its root is the dominant 7th of D major or D minor (depending on the key signature). Remember that the dominant 7th of a minor key has an accidental because it contains the raised leading note.

**Positions of Dominant 7th Chords**

When the *root* of the dominant 7th is the lowest note, the chord is in *root position.*

When the *third* is the lowest note, the chord is in *first inversion.*

When the the *fifth* is the lowest note, the chord is in *second inversion.*

When the *seventh* is the lowest note, the chord is in *third inversion.*

Arabic numbers are used to symbolize the intervals formed between the lowest note of the chord and the upper notes. Abbreviated versions of these numbers are included in chord symbols, as shown in the example below:

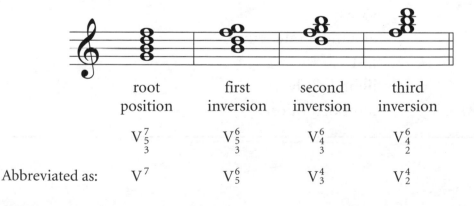

| | root position | first inversion | second inversion | third inversion |
|---|---|---|---|---|
| | $V^7_5 {}_3$ | $V^6_5 {}_3$ | $V^6_4 {}_3$ | $V^6_4 {}_2$ |
| Abbreviated as: | $V^7$ | $V^6_5$ | $V^4_3$ | $V^4_2$ |

**A** 1. Write dominant 7th chords and their inversions in the following keys. Use chord symbols to identify the position of each chord.

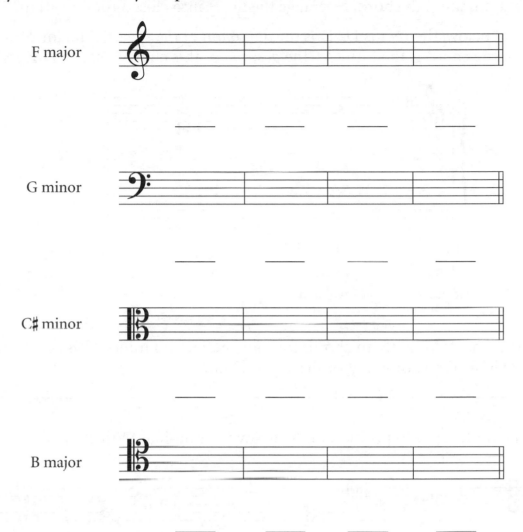

**A**

The dominant 7th chord can be written in open position. The three upper notes may occur in any order. The bottom note determines the position of the chord.

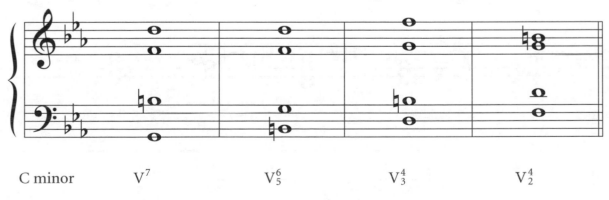

C minor          $V^7$          $V^6_5$          $V^4_3$          $V^4_2$

# THE DOMINANT 7TH CHORD

You may be asked to name the root, key, and position of a dominant 7th chord. To identify a dominant 7th chord, rearrange the notes into closed root position.

In the example below, the *root* is D. D is the *dominant of the key* of G major. Since the lowest note of the chord is the fifth (A), the *position* of this chord is second inversion.

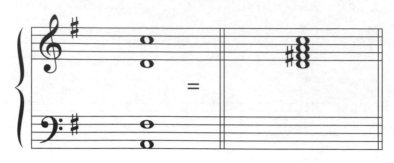

| | |
|---|---|
| root: | D |
| key: | G major |
| position: | 2nd inversion |

Remember that the dominant 7th chords for tonic major and minor keys are the same. In this case, D is also the dominant of the key of G minor.

---

1.   Name the root, key, and position of the following dominant 7th chords.

root: _____   _____   _____   _____   _____   _____

key: _____   _____   _____   _____   _____   _____

position: _____   _____   _____   _____   _____   _____

root: _____   _____   _____   _____   _____   _____

key: _____   _____   _____   _____   _____   _____

position: _____   _____   _____   _____   _____   _____

2.  Name the root, key, and position of the following dominant 7th chords.

root:  _____  _____  _____  _____  _____

key:  _____  _____  _____  _____  _____

position:  _____  _____  _____  _____  _____

root:  _____  _____  _____  _____  _____

key:  _____  _____  _____  _____  _____

position:  _____  _____  _____  _____  _____

root:  _____  _____  _____  _____  _____

key:  _____  _____  _____  _____  _____

position:  _____  _____  _____  _____  _____

# THE DOMINANT 7TH CHORD

**A**

## Inversions

You may be asked to write four dominant 7th chords (in root position, first inversion, second inversion, and third inversion) using a given note as the lowest note for each chord.

In the example below, G is the given note.

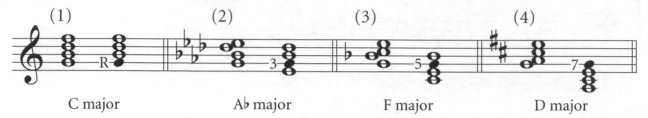

1. The given note G is used as the *root* of a dominant 7th chord. This chord is the dominant 7th of C major.

2. The given note G is used as the *third* of a dominant 7th chord. The root of this chord is E flat, so this chord is the *first inversion* of the dominant 7th of A flat major.

3. The given note G is used as the *fifth* of a dominant 7th chord. The root of this chord is C, so this chord is the *second inversion* of the dominant 7th of F major.

4. The given note G is used as the *seventh* of a dominant 7th chord. The root of this chord is A, so this chord is the *third inversion* of the dominant 7th of D major.

1. Write four different dominant 7th chords (root position and inversions) using D as the lowest note. Name the major key for each chord.

2. Write four different dominant 7th chords (root position and inversions) using F as the lowest note. Name the major key for each chord.

3. Write four different dominant 7th chords (root position and inversions) using A as the lowest note. Name the minor key for each chord.

4. Add accidentals to the following chords to make dominant 7th chords.
   Name two keys for each chord.

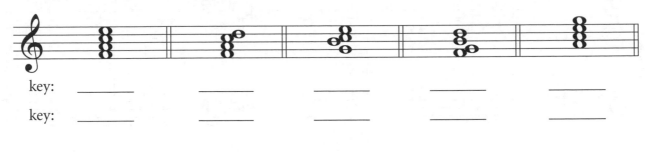

key: _____   _____   _____   _____   _____

key: _____   _____   _____   _____   _____

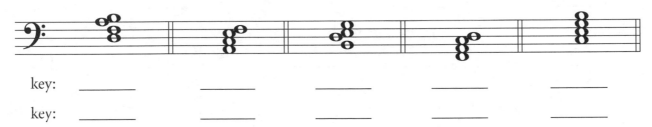

key: _____   _____   _____   _____   _____

key: _____   _____   _____   _____   _____

5. Write the following dominant 7th chords in the bass clef, using key signatures:
   (a) root position of the dominant 7th of G♭ major
   (b) first inversion of the dominant 7th of B minor
   (c) second inversion of the dominant 7th of C♯ minor
   (d) third inversion of the dominant 7th of F minor
   (e) first inversion of the dominant 7th of D♭ major

   (a)            (b)            (c)            (d)            (e)

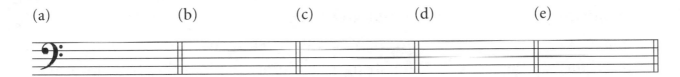

6. Write four different dominant 7th chords (root position and inversions) using E
   as the lowest note. Name two keys for each chord.

key: _____      _____      _____      _____

key: _____      _____      _____      _____

# THE DOMINANT 7TH CHORD

7.  Name the root, key, and position of the following dominant 7th chords.

root: _____    _____    _____    _____  _____

key: _____    _____    _____    _____  _____

position: _____    _____    _____    _____  _____

8.  Learn the following Italian terms and their definitions.

**A**

| | |
|---|---|
| *agitato* | agitated |
| *arco* | for stringed instruments: resume bowing after a *pizzicato* passage |
| *calando* | becoming slower and softer |
| *con grazia* | with grace |
| *dolente* | sad |
| *grandioso* | grand, grandiose |
| *martellato* | strongly accented, hammered |
| *pizzicato* | for stringed instruments: pluck the string instead of bowing |
| *quindicesima alta (15ma)* | two octaves higher |
| *secondo, seconda* | second; second or lower part of a duet |

# THE DIMINISHED 7TH CHORD

**A** The **diminished 7th chord** is a 7th chord built on the raised leading note of a minor key.

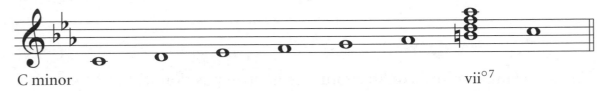

C minor        vii°7

The chord symbol for the diminished 7th is vii°7.

vii°7 is made up of a diminished triad plus a diminished 7th above the root.

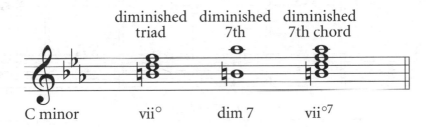

|  | diminished triad | diminished 7th | diminished 7th chord |
|--|--|--|--|
| C minor | vii° | dim 7 | vii°7 |

vii°7 may also be thought of as a stack of three minor 3rds.

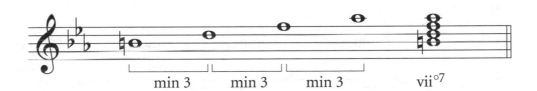

min 3     min 3     min 3     vii°7

Diminished 7ths can occur in root position and three inversions. The inversions are symbolized the same way as the dominant 7th inversions.

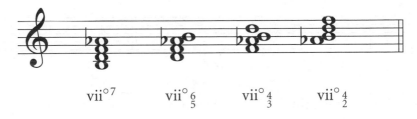

vii°7     vii°$\frac{6}{5}$     vii°$\frac{4}{3}$     vii°$\frac{4}{2}$

# THE DIMINISHED 7TH CHORD

1. Name the key and write the chord symbol for the following diminished 7th chords.

chord: _____  _____  _____  _____  _____  _____  _____  _____

key: _____  _____  _____  _____  _____  _____  _____  _____

2. The following diminished 7th chords are in open position without a key signature. Name the key and write the chord symbol for each.

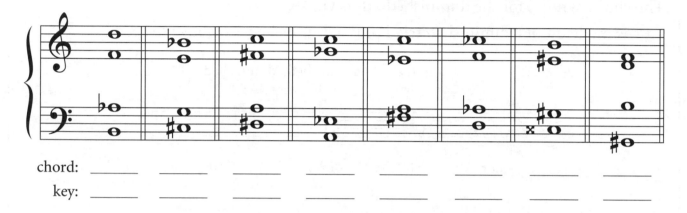

chord: _____  _____  _____  _____  _____  _____  _____  _____

key: _____  _____  _____  _____  _____  _____  _____  _____

3. Using key signatures, write diminished 7th chords in root position in the following keys.

A minor   B minor   F minor   C♯ minor   G minor

E minor   B♭ minor   F♯ minor   D♯ minor   E♭ minor

D minor   A♯ minor   A♭ minor   C minor   G♯ minor

**A**    4.    Learn the definitions of the following chord types.

| | | |
|---|---|---|
| triad | chord consisting of a root, 3rd, and 5th | |
| 7th chord | chord consisting of a root, 3rd, 5th, and 7th | |
| quartal chord | chord built on a series of 4ths | |
| cluster | chord consisting of a combination of at least three adjacent notes of any scale | |
| polychord | combination of two or more different chords | |

5.    Learn the following Italian terms and their meanings.

**A**

| | |
|---|---|
| *semplice* | simple |
| *sforzando,* **sf**, **sfz** | a sudden, strong accent of a single note or chord |
| *simile* | continue in the same manner as has just been indicated |
| *sostenuto* | sustained |
| *sotto voce* | soft, subdued, under the breath |

# Ⓘ Ⓐ CADENCES

A **cadence** is a place of rest in music. Cadences are two-chord progressions that occur at the ends of phrases and at the end of a piece of music. There are two types of cadences: *final* and *non-final*.

**The Perfect Cadence**

The **perfect cadence** is the most common cadence. It consists of the dominant triad moving to the tonic triad (V–I). Since it ends on the tonic, it is considered to be a *final* cadence.

Cadences in the keyboard style are written with the root of each chord in the bass clef, and the root, third, and fifth of each chord in the treble clef in close position. Perfect cadences in minor keys are much the same as those in major keys, except that in a minor key, the leading note in the dominant chord must be raised. All perfect cadences in minor keys have an accidental in the dominant chord.

A perfect cadence most often occurs over two measures, with the dominant chord on the last (or second last) beat of the first measure and the tonic chord on the first beat of the second measure.

Study the following perfect cadences.

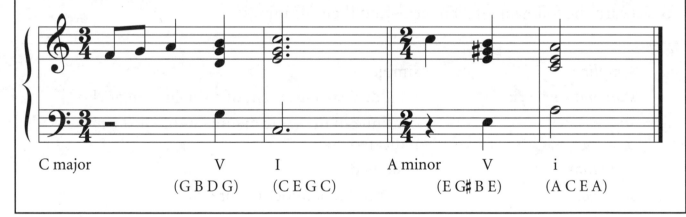

C major            V      I          A minor     V     i

(G B D G)    (C E G C)          (E G♯ B E)    (A C E A)

The progression V⁷–I is also a perfect cadence. In this progression, the dominant 7th can be written as a complete chord with the root in the bass and third, fifth, and seventh in the treble. It may also be written as an incomplete chord, leaving out the fifth, with the root in the bass and a doubled root, third, and seventh in the treble. In some four-part writing, the seventh of V⁷ must fall to the third of the I chord. In keyboard and instrumental style, this is not necessary.

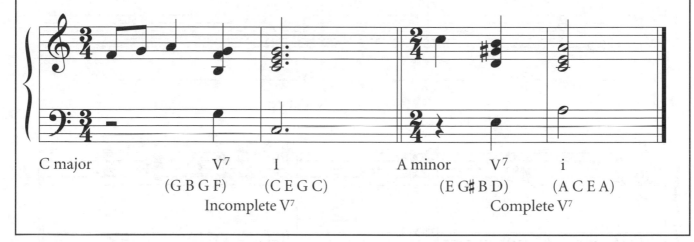

## The Plagal Cadence

In **plagal cadences,** the subdominant chord moves to the tonic chord (IV–I). Like the perfect cadence, the plagal cadence is a final cadence because it ends on the tonic. It most often occurs over two measures, with the subdominant chord on the last beat of the first measure, and the tonic chord on the first beat of the second measure. Plagal cadences often harmonize the "Amen" at the end of a hymn.

Study the following plagal cadences.

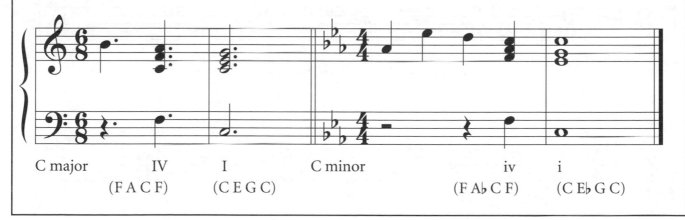

# CADENCES

1.  For the following chord progressions, name the key, name the cadence (perfect or plagal), and symbolize the chords (V–I or IV–I).

key:_____    _____    _____          key:_____    _____    _____

cadence:_____          cadence:_____


key:_____    _____    _____          key:_____    _____    _____

cadence:_____          cadence:_____


key:_____    _____    _____          key:_____    _____    _____

cadence:_____          cadence:_____


key:_____    _____    _____          key:_____    _____    _____

cadence:_____          cadence:_____

2. For each of the following, name the key, name the cadence (perfect or plagal), and symbolize the chords (V–I or IV–I).

key:_____   _____   _____          key:_____   _____   _____

cadence:_____          cadence:_____

key:_____   _____   _____          key:_____   _____   _____

cadence:_____          cadence:_____

key:_____   _____   _____          key:_____   _____   _____

cadence:_____          cadence:_____

key:_____   _____   _____          key:_____   _____   _____

cadence:_____          cadence:_____

# CADENCES

key:_____  _____  _____         key:_____  _____  _____

cadence:_____                 cadence:_____

key:_____  _____  _____         key:_____  _____  _____

cadence:_____                 cadence:_____

key:_____  _____  _____         key:_____  _____  _____

cadence:_____                 cadence:_____

key:_____  _____  _____         key:_____  _____  _____

cadence:_____                 cadence:_____

## The Imperfect Cadence

So far, we have learned two types of cadences: the perfect cadence (V–I or V⁷–I) and the plagal cadence (IV–I). Because these cadences end on the tonic chord, they give a sense of completeness or finality, like the period at the end of a sentence. They are often used at the end of a piece of music.

The **imperfect cadence** has an unfinished sound—like a comma, rather than a period. The imperfect cadence is also known as a **half close**. The second chord of an imperfect cadence is always the dominant (V) chord. The first chord may be one of many. The chords that we will use before the dominant in this lesson are the tonic (I) and the subdominant (IV). Therefore, the two imperfect cadences that we will study are I–V and IV–V. In an imperfect cadence, the first chord (I or IV) is usually on a weaker beat, and the dominant chord is on a stronger beat.

Study the imperfect cadences below.

Imperfect cadences in the minor key contain the raised leading note in the V chord.

# CADENCES

1. For each of the following, name the key, name the cadence (perfect, plagal, or imperfect), and symbolize the chords.

key:_____ _____ _____    key:_____ _____ _____

cadence:_____    cadence:_____

key:_____ _____ _____    key:_____ _____    key:_____

cadence:_____    cadence:_____

key:_____ _____ _____    key:_____ _____ _____

cadence:_____    cadence:_____

key:_____ _____ _____    key:_____ _____ _____

cadence:_____    cadence:_____

key:_____    _____ _____          key:_____    _____ _____

cadence:_____                    cadence:_____

key:_____    _____ _____          key:_____    _____ _____

cadence:_____                    cadence:_____

key:_____    _____ _____          key:_____    _____ _____

cadence:_____                    cadence:_____

key:_____    _____ _____          key:_____    _____ _____

cadence:_____                    cadence:_____

# CADENCES

### Writing Perfect Cadences

There are five steps for writing perfect cadences in keyboard style:

1.  Write the key signature, then write the roots of the dominant and tonic triads of that key in the bass clef. The dominant note may either rise a 4th or fall a 5th to the tonic note. Identify the key and write the chord progression (using Roman numerals) below the bass staff. (Note: You may also find it helpful to write the notes of each chord under the symbols.)

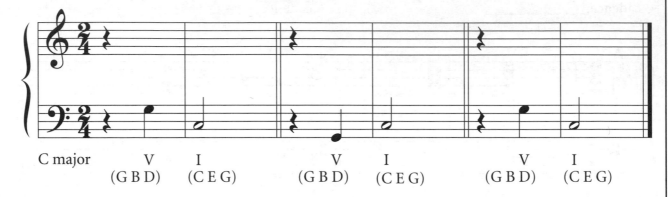

C major    V     I            V     I            V     I
             (G B D) (C E G)     (G B D) (C E G)     (G B D) (C E G)

2.  Write one of the notes of the dominant triad (root, third, or fifth) in the treble clef.

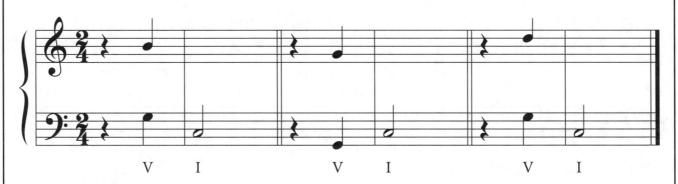

V     I            V     I            V     I

3.  Complete the dominant triad by adding the remaining two notes under the treble note.

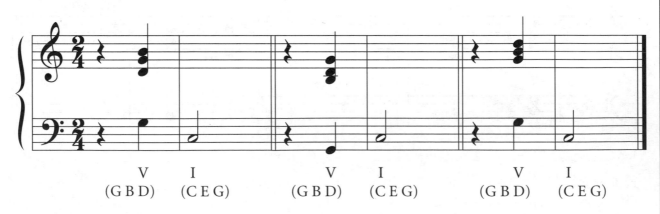

V     I            V     I            V     I
(G B D) (C E G)     (G B D) (C E G)     (G B D) (C E G)

4. There is a common tone between the dominant and tonic triads. A common tone is a note that is the same in both chords. Copy that common tone at the same pitch above the tonic bass note.

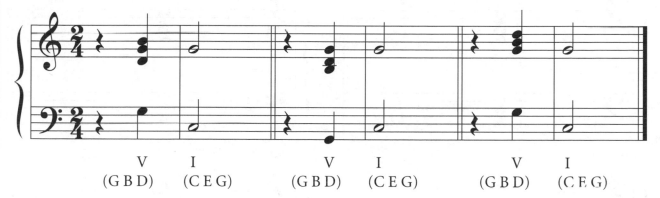

|  | V | I |  | V | I |  | V | I |
|---|---|---|---|---|---|---|---|---|
|  | (G B D) | (C E G) |  | (G B D) | (C E G) |  | (G B D) | (C E G) |

5. Add the remaining two notes, keeping the shift from the dominant to the tonic chord as smooth as possible. Usually, these two notes move up one step.

|  | V | I |  | V | I |  | V | I |
|---|---|---|---|---|---|---|---|---|

**A**

### Writing Perfect Cadences in Minor Keys

Writing perfect cadences in minor keys is virtually the same as writing them in major keys. Follow the same steps as for writing a perfect cadence above, but remember the following.

In a minor key, the leading note in the dominant chord must be raised. This means that the dominant chord will always have an accidental.

Study the following examples of perfect cadences in both major and minor keys.

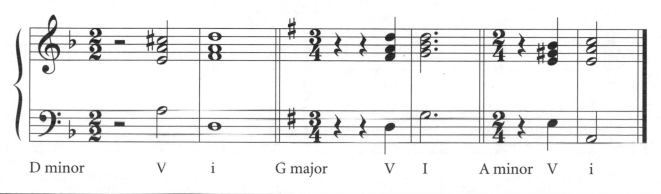

| D minor | V | i | G major | V | I | A minor | V | i |
|---------|---|---|---------|---|---|---------|---|---|

# CADENCES

1. Write two-measure examples of perfect cadences in the following keys, using key signatures. Add rests where necessary to complete the final measures.

B minor                                    D♭ major

A major                                    C minor

F♯ minor                                   E♭ major

D major                                    C♯ minor

B major                                    G minor

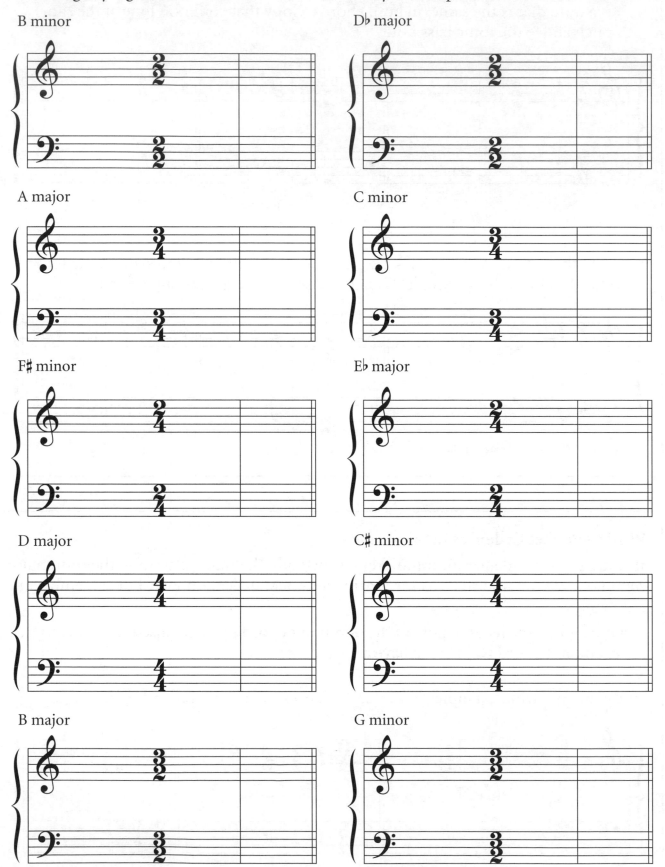

*THE COMPLETE ELEMENTARY MUSIC RUDIMENTS*

**Writing Plagal Cadences**

There are five steps for writing plagal cadences in keyboard style:

1.  Write the key signature, then write the roots of the subdominant and tonic triads of that key in the bass clef. The subdominant note may either rise a 5th or fall a 4th to the tonic note. Identify the key and write the chord progression (using Roman numerals) below the bass staff. (Note: You may also find it helpful to write the notes of each chord under the symbols.)

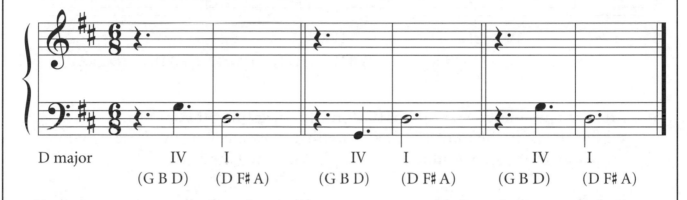

2.  Write one of the notes of the subdominant triad (root, third, or the fifth) in the treble clef.

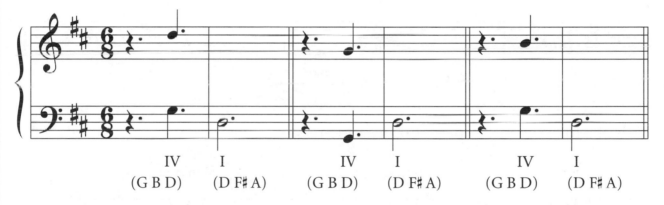

3.  Complete the subdominant triad by adding the remaining two notes under the treble note.

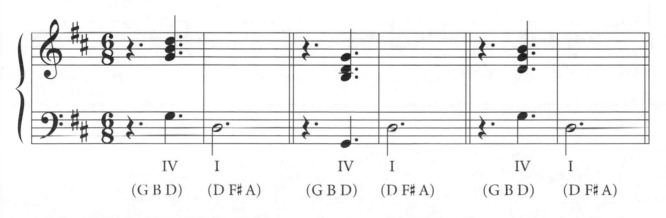

4.  There is a common tone between the subdominant and tonic triads. Copy that common tone at the same pitch above the tonic bass note.

5.  Add the remaining two notes of the tonic triad, keeping the shift from the subdominant to the tonic chord as smooth as possible. Usually, these two notes move down one step. Add rests to complete the final measure.

Study the following examples of plagal cadences.

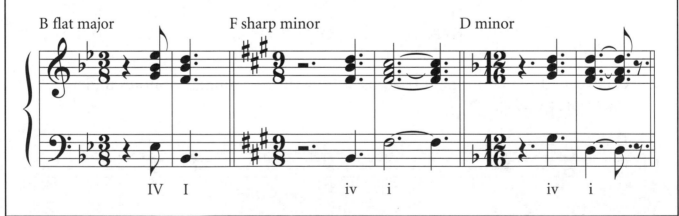

**A** 1. Write two-measure examples of plagal cadences in the following keys, using key signatures. Add rests where necessary to complete the final measures.

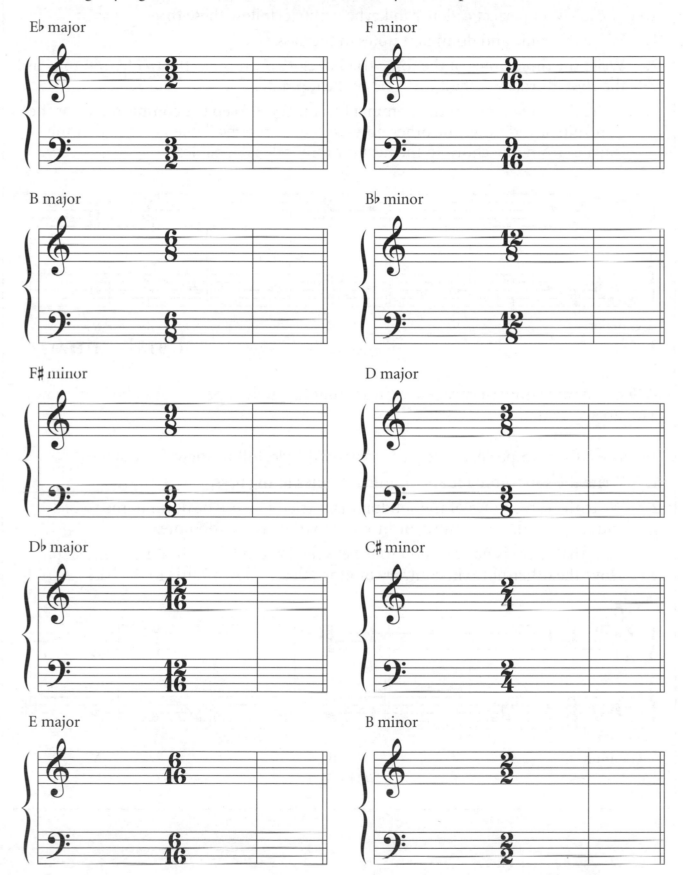

E♭ major

F minor

B major

B♭ minor

F♯ minor

D major

D♭ major

C♯ minor

E major

B minor

# CADENCES

### Writing Imperfect Cadences

To write a I–V imperfect cadence in keyboard style, follow these three steps:

1.  Write the tonic and dominant notes in the bass.

2.  Write the three notes of the tonic triad in close position in the treble. You may use the root, third, or fifth of the triad as the top note.

3.  Write the three notes of the dominant triad. Try to keep the common tone at the same pitch, and move the other notes to the nearest available notes so that the transfer from one chord to the next is as smooth as possible.

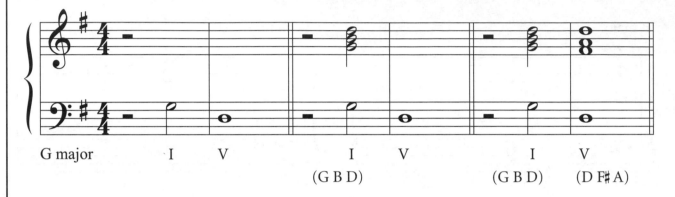

G major       I    V             I    V            I    V

                                (G B D)           (G B D)   (D F♯ A)

When you write imperfect cadences in a minor key, remember to raise the leading note with an accidental.

To write a IV–V imperfect cadence in keyboard style, follow these three steps:

1.  Write the subdominant and dominant notes in the bass.

2.  Write the three notes of the subdominant triad in close position in the treble. You may use the root, third, or fifth of the triad as the top note.

3.  Note that there is no common tone between IV and V. The bass rises one step. Move the other notes in contrary motion (that is, downward) to the bass.

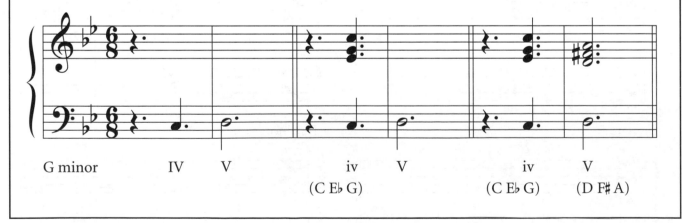

G minor       IV    V            iv    V           iv    V

                                (C E♭ G)         (C E♭ G)   (D F♯ A)

Study the following examples of imperfect cadences.

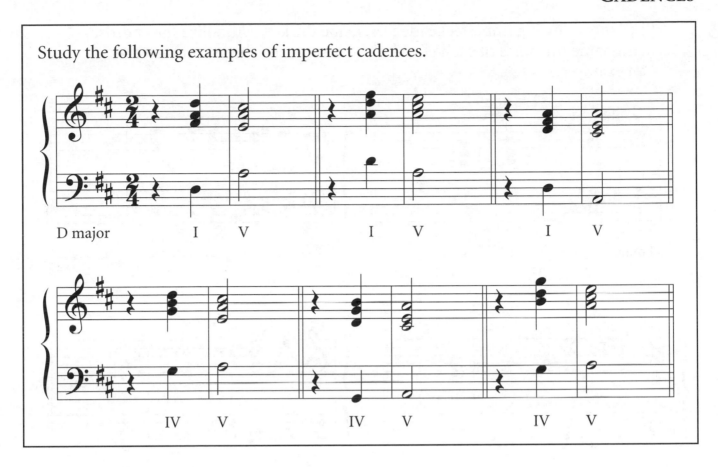

## CADENCES

1. For the following imperfect cadences, name the key, symbolize the chords, and name the notes of each chord. (The first one has been completed as an example.)

G major         I     V

(G B D)    (D F♯ A)

Key:____     _____    _____

Key:____     _____    _____

Key:____     _____    _____

Key:____     _____    _____

Key:____     _____    _____

Key:____     _____    _____

2. Complete imperfect cadences above the following bass notes. Name the key, symbolize the chords, and name the notes of each chord.

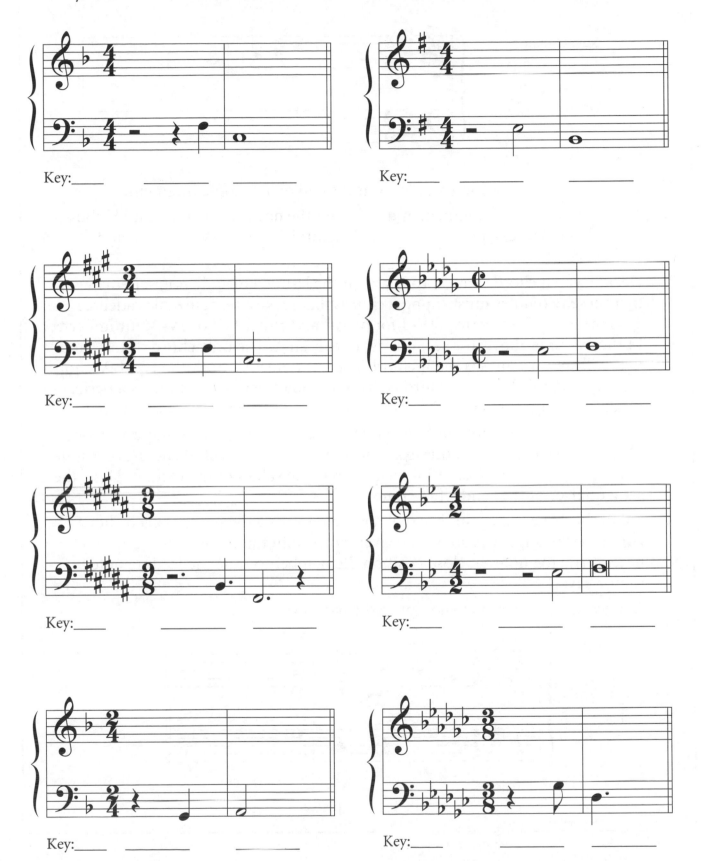

Key:____    ____    ____    ____

Key:____    ____    ____    ____

Key:____    ____    ____    ____

Key:____    ____    ____    ____

Key:____    ____    ____    ____

Key:____    ____    ____    ____

# CADENCES

## Adding Cadences at the End of a Melodic Fragment

Key: G major
I  =  G B D
IV =  C E G
V  =  D F♯ A

These are the steps for writing a cadence at the end of a melodic fragment:

1. Name the key of the fragment and write out the notes of the I, IV, and V chords for that key. The example above is in G major: I = G B D, IV = C E G, and V = D F♯ A.

2. Decide which chords are appropriate for the last two melody notes. Remember that these two notes must support chords that make a recognizable cadence. This means V–I for perfect, IV–I for plagal, and either I–V or IV–V for imperfect. In the example above, the second-last note is an A. The only chord of I, IV, and V that will support an A is the V chord. The last note is G. Both the I and IV chords can support a G, but the I chord is the only choice here since it forms a perfect cadence. Using IV would not create a recognizable cadence, so it is not an option.

3. Write the chord symbols and the name of the cadence (perfect, imperfect, or plagal) below the staff. In this example, it is V–I and perfect. Write the bass notes of the chords in the bass staff matching the note values of the melody. Here, they are a quarter note D and whole note G.

4. Fill in the upper voices in the treble staff completing the notes of each chord. Do not write any notes above the given notes. Join the stems to the given melody note. Write the notes in close position. Remember to raise the leading note in minor keys.

5. Add the necessary rests to complete the bass line.

G major                    V    I
                         perfect

Study these examples of cadences at the end of melodic fragments.

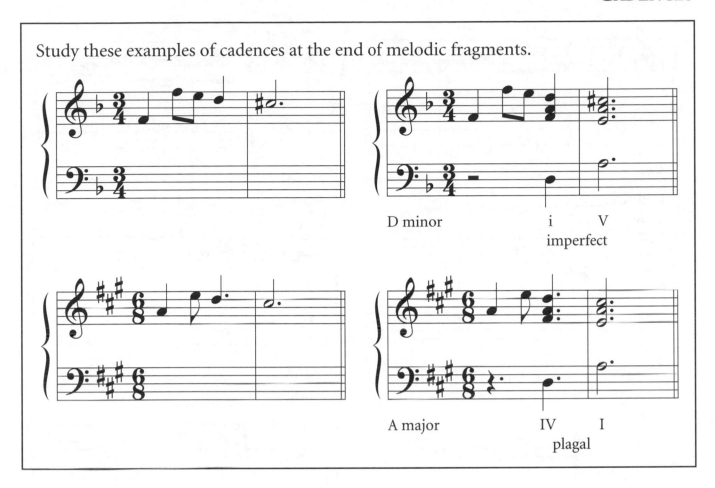

1. For the following melodic fragments, name the key and write an appropriate cadence at the end. Symbolize the chords and identify the cadences as perfect, plagal, or imperfect.

Key:____  _____          _____

Cadence:_____

Key:____  _____          _____

Cadence:_____

Key:____  _____          _____

Cadence:_____

Key:____  _____          _____

Cadence:_____

## CADENCES

Key:____ ____ ____

Cadence:_____

Key:____ ____ ____

Cadence:_____

Key:____ ____ ____

Cadence:_____

Key:____ ____ ____

Cadence:_____

Key:____ ____ ____

Cadence:_____

Key:____ ____ ____

Cadence:_____

Key:____ ____ ____

Cadence:_____

Key:____ ____ ____

Cadence:_____

Key:____ ____ ____

Cadence:_____

Key:____ ____ ____

Cadence:_____

Key:____  _____  _____  _____

Cadence:_____

Key:____  _____  _____

Cadence:_____

Key:____  _____  _____  _____

Cadence:_____

Key:____  _____  _____

Cadence:_____

Key:____  _____  _____  _____

Cadence:_____

Key:____  _____  _____  _____

Cadence:_____

Key:____  _____  _____  _____

Cadence:_____

Key:____  _____  _____  _____

Cadence:_____

2.  Learn the following German terms and their definitions.

**A**

| *bewegt* | agitated, excited |
| *langsam* | slow |
| *mässig* | moderate, moderately |
| *mit Ausdruck* | with expression |
| *schnell* | fast |
| *sehr* | very |

# FINDING THE KEY OF A MELODY

Ⓑ
Ⓘ
Ⓐ

Most music is written in a specific key or tonality. If the music has a key signature, it is fairly easy to determine the key. The key signature tells us that the music can be one of two keys: a major key or its relative minor. Music in minor keys usually has accidentals to indicate the raised seventh degree.

The following melody has two sharps in the key signature, and there are no other accidentals. Therefore, the melody is in the key of D major.

This melody has a key signature of two flats, indicating B flat major or its relative minor, G minor. The melody also contains an F sharp, indicating the raised seventh of a minor key. Therefore, the melody is in G minor.

It is possible for a melody in a minor key to have two accidentals, indicating the raised sixth and seventh that are found in the melodic minor scale.

1.  Name the keys of the following melodies.

Traditional carol

key: _____

Arcangelo Corelli
(1653–1713)

key: _____

Johann Sebastian Bach
(1685–1750)

key: _____

Henry Purcell
(1659–1695)

key: _____

Edvard Grieg
(1843–1907)

key: _____

Wolfgang Amadeus Mozart
(1756–1791)

key: _____

Henri Bertini
(1798–1876)

key: _____

Franz Joseph Haydn
(1732–1809)

key: _____

# Finding the Key of a Melody

## Accidentals

An accidental is a sign placed before a note to alter its pitch. Accidentals apply only to the note before which they are written. They do not alter the same note written at another octave.

An accidental lasts throughout a measure unless cancelled by another accidental. A bar line cancels an accidental except when the altered note is tied into the next measure. In this case, the tied note is the only note affected by the accidental.

### Finding the Key of a Melody that Has No Key Signature

The following melody contains a number of accidentals, but it has no key signature. How can we determine the key of this melody?

1. List the accidentals of the melody in the order in which they would appear in a key signature. This melody contains two flats: B flat and E flat.

2. Name the key signature. *Hints: If all the accidentals in the melody fit into a key signature, the melody is probably major. Often, but not always, a melody ends on the tonic note.*

   B flat and E flat are the first two flats in a flat key signature. The major key containing two flats is B flat major. Since there are no other accidentals, we can conclude that this melody is in B flat major. Another clue is that the melody ends on B flat.

Here is the melody written with a key signature:

1.  List the accidentals and name the keys of the following melodies.
    Rewrite the melodies using key signatures.

accidentals: _____

key: _____

accidentals: _____

key: _____

accidentals: _____

key: _____

# Finding the Key of a Melody

Sometimes the accidentals in a melody do not form a recognizable key signature. If this is the case, there is a good chance that the melody is in a minor key.

1.  This melody contains three flats:  B flat, A flat, and D flat.

2.  This could be the key signature of A flat major (four flats) but E flat is missing. The E in this melody could be the raised leading note of F minor. The key signature of F minor is four flats. (F minor is the relative minor of A flat major.) Another clue is that the melody begins and ends on F.

    (Hint: If one note in a melody is raised, that note is often, but not always, the leading note of a minor key.)

Here is the melody written with a key signature:

Here are two more examples:

1.  This melody contains three sharps:  F sharp, C sharp, and A sharp.

2.  This could be the key signature of D major (two sharps) but we also have to explain the A sharp. The A sharp in this melody could be the raised leading note of B minor. The key signature of B minor is two sharps. (B minor is the relative minor of D major.) Another clue is that the melody ends on B.

1.  This melody contains five sharps:  F double sharp, C sharp, G sharp, D sharp, and A sharp.

2.  This could be the key signature of B major (five sharps) but we also have to explain the F double sharp. F double sharp in this melody could be the raised leading note of G sharp minor. G sharp minor is the relative minor of B major, and has the same key signature (five sharps). Another clue is that the melody ends on G sharp.

*The Complete Elementary Music Rudiments*

The last two examples on the previous page demonstrate two more helpful hints.

In minor key signatures of up to four sharps, there is always a skip of two sharps from the last sharp of the key signature to the leading note. In minor melodies with a key signature of five or more sharps, the raised leading note is always a double sharp.

There is another variation to watch for. In a minor key, the sixth degree (submediant) may also be raised. If both the sixth and seventh degrees of the scale are raised, this indicates the melodic form of the minor scale.

Remember that a melody may be in a minor key if:

1.  The melody contains both sharps and flats.

2.  The melody contains both sharps and double sharps.

3.  The melody contains both flats and naturals.

2.  List the accidentals and name the keys of the following melodies.
    Rewrite the melodies using key signatures.

# Finding the Key of a Melody

Edvard Grieg
(1843–1907)

accidentals: _____

key: _____

Edward MacDowell
(1860–1908)

accidentals: _____

key: _____

Franz Schubert
(1797–1828)

accidentals: _____

key: _____

Pyotr Il'yich Tchaikovsky
(1840–1893)

accidentals: _____

key: _____

*The Complete Elementary Music Rudiments*

**Finding a Scale From a Given Group of Chords**

You may be asked to identify a scale or scales (major, natural minor, or harmonic minor) in which a group of chords is found. To do this, follow these steps:

1.  If the given chords use a key signature, identify the major key and its relative minor.

2.  Look for accidentals that are not part of the key signature. They are usually the raised leading note of the harmonic minor scale.

3.  If there is no key signature given, collect all the accidentals and see if they form a recognizable key signature. If there are missing or extra accidentals, the chords may be part of a harmonic minor scale.

4.  Using the information you have collected, name the scale or scales in which the chords are found.

Study the following examples.

For this group of chords, accidentals are used instead of a key signature. The accidentals found in these chords are E flat and A flat. If the scale in which all of these chords are found was a major or natural minor scale, B would be flat also. The B is natural because it is the raised leading note of the scale of C minor harmonic.

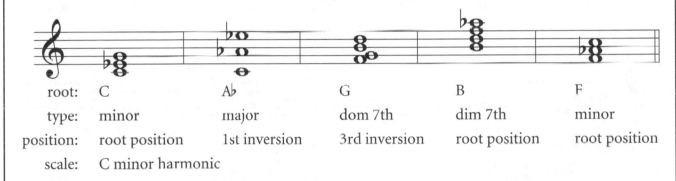

| root: | C | A♭ | G | B | F |
|---|---|---|---|---|---|
| type: | minor | major | dom 7th | dim 7th | minor |
| position: | root position | 1st inversion | 3rd inversion | root position | root position |
| scale: | C minor harmonic | | | | |

All of these chords can be built on the notes of the scale of C minor harmonic. C minor is i, A flat major is VI, G dominant 7th is V7, B dim 7th is vii°⁷, and F minor is iv.

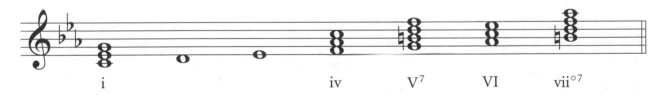

In this next example, if we collect all the accidentals contained in the given chords, we find B flat, E flat, A flat, and D flat. This forms a recognizable key signature. All of these accidentals can be found in the scale of A flat major and its relative natural minor, F natural minor. These chords can be found in both scales. It is important to note that if a group of chords can be found in a major scale, they will also be found in that major scale's relative natural minor.

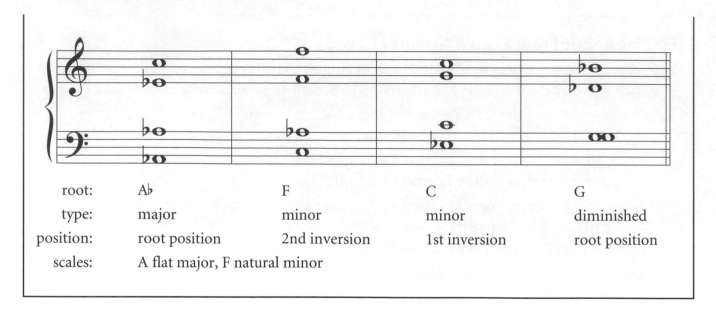

| root: | A♭ | F | C | G |
|---|---|---|---|---|
| type: | major | minor | minor | diminished |
| position: | root position | 2nd inversion | 1st inversion | root position |
| scales: | A flat major, F natural minor | | | |

1. Write the above chords in root position on the correct notes of the following scales. Write Roman numerals under each.

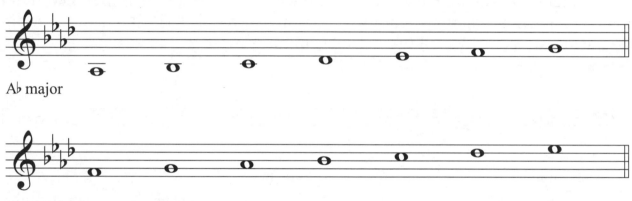

A♭ major

F natural minor

2. For the following chords: name the rote, quality, and position. Name the scale or scales which contain all of the chords.

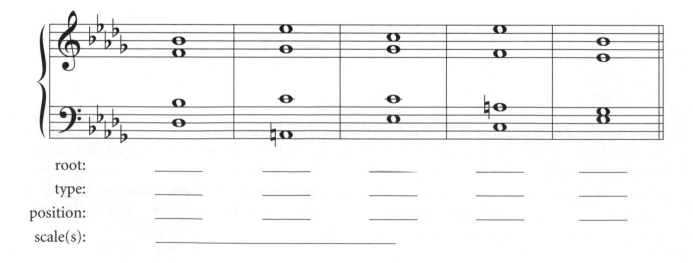

root: _____ _____ _____ _____ _____

type: _____ _____ _____ _____ _____

position: _____ _____ _____ _____ _____

scale(s): _____

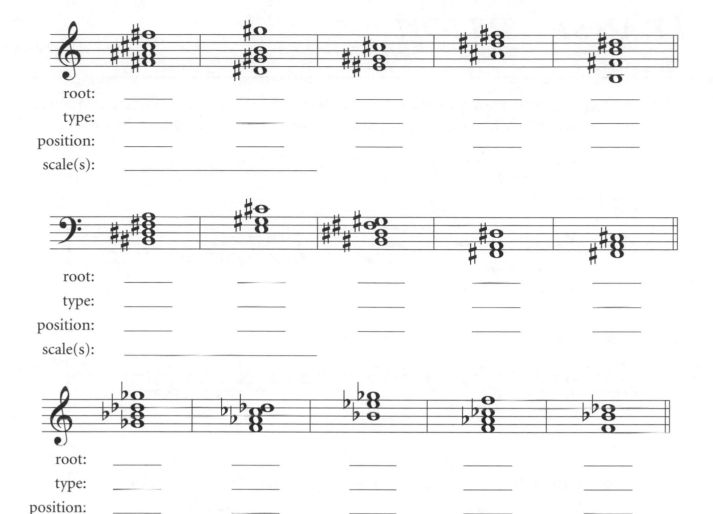

root: _____ _____ _____ _____ _____

type: _____ _____ _____ _____ _____

position: _____ _____ _____ _____ _____

scale(s): _____

root: _____ _____ _____ _____ _____

type: _____ _____ _____ _____ _____

position: _____ _____ _____ _____ _____

scale(s): _____

root: _____ _____ _____ _____ _____

type: _____ _____ _____ _____ _____

position: _____ _____ _____ _____ _____

scale(s): _____

3. Learn the following Italian terms and their meanings.

**A**

| | |
|---|---|
| *stringendo* | pressing, becoming faster |
| *subito* | suddenly |
| *tacet* | be silent |
| *tutti* | a passage for the ensemble |
| *vivo* | lively |
| *volta* | time (for example, *prima volta*, first time; *seconda volta*, second time) |
| *volti subito, v.s.* | turn the page quickly |

# TRANSPOSITION

In basic rudiments, **transposition** involves writing melodies at a different octave. Melodies can be written an octave higher or lower in the same clef or in a different clef.

Here is a melody:

Here is the same melody transposed up one octave in the same clef:

Here is the original melody transposed down one octave into the bass clef:

Remember that when you transpose a melody up or down an octave, the key remains the same.

If you transpose a melody down one octave, use the same key signature and move each note down the interval of a perfect octave.

If you transpose a melody up one octave, use the same key signature and move each note up the interval of a perfect octave.

If you transpose a melody one octave into a different clef, remember to include the new clef and to write the key signature in the new clef. Be careful when deciding where the new melody will begin, and don't forget to change the direction of the stems if necessary.

1. Name the key of this melody. Transpose it down one octave in the treble clef.

key:_____

2. Name the key of this melody. Transpose it up one octave in the treble clef.

key:_____

3. Name the key of this melody. Transpose it up one octave in the bass clef.

key:_____

4. Name the key of this melody. Transpose it down one octave in the bass clef.

key:_____

# TRANSPOSITION

5. Name the key of this melody. Transpose it down one octave into the bass clef.

key:_____

6. Name the key of this melody. Transpose it down one octave into the bass clef.

key:_____

7. Name the key of this melody. Transpose it up one octave into the treble clef.

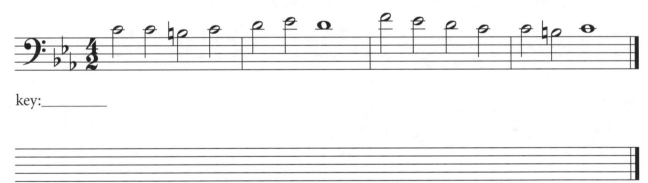

key:_____

8. Name the key of this melody. Transpose it up one octave into the treble clef.

key:_____

9.  Name the key of this melody. Transpose it down one octave into the bass clef.

key:_____

10. Name the key of this melody. Transpose it up one octave in the treble clef.

key:_____

11. Name the key of this melody. Rewrite it in the treble clef at the same pitch.

key:_____

12. Name the key of this melody. Rewrite it in the bass clef at the same pitch.

key:_____

# TRANSPOSITION

### Transposing to a New Key

**Transposition** may also involve writing or playing music at a different pitch or in a different key. Here we will learn to transpose a melody from one major key to another major key.

To transpose a melody into a new key, you must know the original key of the melody and either the new key or the interval of transposition. If the interval of transposition is given, you must determine the new key.

Here is a melody in G major:

To transpose this melody up a major 3rd, follow these four steps:

1. Determine the original key.
   The original key is G major.

2. Find the note that is a major 3rd above G. This note will be the tonic of the new key.
   A major 3rd above G is B. The new key will be B major.

3. Write the key signature of the new key.
   B major has a key signature of five sharps.

4. Move each note in the original melody up a 3rd. (Note that because we have used the key signature of the new key, every one of these 3rds will be a major 3rd.)

Here is the melody transposed into B major.

If a melody contains accidentals, the transposed melody will also contain accidentals. If a note in the original melody is raised, the corresponding transposed note must be raised. If a note in the original melody is lowered, the corresponding transposed note must be lowered.

In the following example, the original melody in B flat major has been transposed up a major 2nd to C major. The original melody contains two accidentals: E natural (m. 2) and B natural (m. 3)—both these notes have been raised one semitone.

B♭ major

This means that the corresponding notes in the transposed melody (F and C) must also be raised one semitone: F sharp (m. 2) and C sharp (m. 3).

C major

1. Name the key of the following melody.

    (a) Transpose it up a perfect 4th and name the new key.

    (b) Transpose it up a minor 3rd and name the new key.

Traditional African

key:_____

(a)

key:_____

(b)

key:_____

# TRANSPOSITION

2. Name the key of the following melody.

   (a) Transpose it up a major 2nd and name the new key.

   (b) Transpose it into the key of F sharp major.

Traditional German

key:_____

(a)

key:_____

(b)

3. Name the key of the following melody.

   (a) Transpose it into the key of B major.

   (b) Transpose it up a major 3rd and name the new key.

Richard Wagner<br>(1813–1883)

key:_____

(a)

(b)

key:_____

4. Name the key of the following melody.
   (a) Transpose it up a perfect 5th and name the new key.
   (b) Transpose it up a major 2nd and name the new key.

George Frideric Handel
(1685–1759)

key:_____

(a)

key:_____

(b)

key:_____

5. Name the key of the following melody.
   (a) Transpose it into the key of D flat major.
   (b) Transpose it up a minor 6th and name the new key.

Franz Schubert
(1797–1828)

key:_____

(a)

(b)

key:_____

# TRANSPOSITION

6. Name the key of the following melody.

   (a) Transpose it up a perfect 4th and name the new key.

   (b) Transpose it into the key of A major

key:_____

(a)

key:_____

(b)

7. Learn the following Italian terms and their definitions.

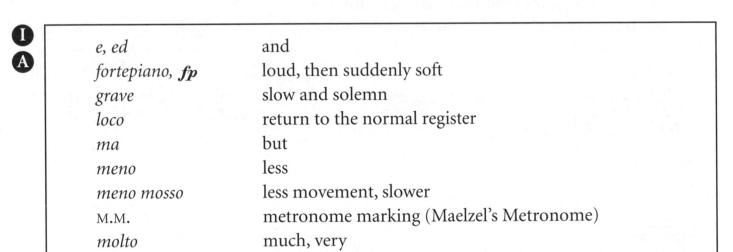

| e, ed | and |
| --- | --- |
| *fortepiano*, **fp** | loud, then suddenly soft |
| *grave* | slow and solemn |
| *loco* | return to the normal register |
| *ma* | but |
| *meno* | less |
| *meno mosso* | less movement, slower |
| M.M. | metronome marking (Maelzel's Metronome) |
| *molto* | much, very |

### Transposing in Minor Keys

Here are four steps to transpose a melody from one minor key to another minor key. (Remember that if a melody is in a minor key, the transposed melody must also be in a minor key.)

Here is a melody that is to be transposed up a major 3rd:

1.  Determine the key of the given melody. This melody is in D minor.

2.  Name the new key. The interval of transposition will determine the new key. A major 3rd above D is F sharp. Therefore the new key is F sharp minor.

major 3rd

3.  Write the key signature of the new key (in this case, three sharps). Move each note in the original melody up a 3rd.

4.  Locate the accidentals in the original melody. These notes must be correspondingly raised or lowered in the transposed version. Here, C sharp (the raised leading note) of the original melody becomes E sharp in the transposed version.

Here is the melody transposed into F sharp minor:

Melodies may also be transposed downwards. For example, if the melody above were to be transposed down a major 2nd, the new key would be C minor.

major 2nd

# TRANSPOSITION

**A**    1.    Transpose the following passages by the given interval. Name the original key and transposed key.

**up a major 3rd**

Johann Sebastian Bach<br>(1685–1750)

original key: _____

transposed key: _____

**up a perfect 4th**

Jean-Philippe Rameau<br>(1683–1764)

original key: _____

transposed key: _____

**up a minor 6th**

Pyotr Il'yich Tchaikovsky<br>(1840–1893)

original key: _____

transposed key: _____

**down a minor 3rd**

Robert Schumann
(1810–1856)

original key: _____

transposed key: _____

---

> **Remember**
>
> A melody in a major key can only be transposed to another major key.
> A melody in a minor key can only be transposed to another minor key.

2. The following passages may be in major or minor keys. Transpose them by the given intervals. Name the original key and transposed key.

**down a diminished 5th**

Johannes Brahms
(1833–1897)

original key: _____

transposed key: _____

**up a major 6th**

Ludwig van Beethoven
(1770–1827)

original key: _____

transposed kcy: _____

# TRANSPOSITION

3. Name the key of the following melody. Transpose it by the following intervals. Name the new keys.

Franz Schubert
(1797–1828)

original key:_____

**up a major 2nd**

transposed key:_____

**down a minor 3rd**

transposed key:_____

**up an augmented 4th**

transposed key:_____

**down a perfect 5th**

transposed key:_____

**down a major 2nd**

transposed key:_____

**up a minor 3rd**

transposed key:_____

4.  Name the key of the following melody. Rewrite it in the clefs listed below.

Franz Schubert
(1797–1828)

key:_____

The alto clef

The tenor clef

5.  Name the key of the following melody. Rewrite it in the clefs listed below.

Antonio Vivaldi
(1678–1741)

key:_____

The alto clef

The tenor clef

6.  Learn the following Italian terms and their definitions.

A

| | |
|---|---|
| *allargando* | broadening, becoming slower |
| *attaca* | proceed without a break |
| *comodo, commodo* | at a comfortable, easy tempo |
| *con sordino* | with mute |
| *largamente* | broadly |
| *l'istesso tempo* | the same tempo |
| *mesto* | sad, mournful |
| *morendo* | dying, fading away |
| *primo, prima* | first; the upper part of a duet |

# TRANSPOSITION FOR ORCHESTRAL INSTRUMENTS

**A**

**S**ome instruments of the orchestra are **transposing instruments.** This means that these instruments produce notes that sound higher or lower than written. The pitch that these instruments actually produce is called **concert pitch.**

For example, when a B-flat instrument plays middle C, it actually produces B flat—a major 2nd lower. Instruments in B flat include the B-flat clarinet, the B-flat trumpet, and the B-flat saxophone.

Here is a passage for B-flat clarinet:

Carl Maria von Weber
(1786–1826)

This is how the passage will sound at concert pitch:

When an instrument in A plays middle C, it actually produces A—a minor 3rd lower. Instruments in A include the A clarinet and the A cornet.

Here is a passage for A cornet:

Edward Elgar
(1857–1934)

This is how the passage will sound at concert pitch:

When an instrument in F plays middle C, it actually produces F—a perfect 5th lower. Instruments in F include the French horn in F and the cor anglais (English horn).

Here is a passage for French horn in F:

Wolfgang Amadeus Mozart
(1756–1791)

This is how the passage will sound at concert pitch:

1. The following excerpt is written at concert pitch. Name the key and transpose the passage into the correct keys for the following instruments. (All instruments sound at the same pitch.) Name the new keys.

Wolfgang Amadeus Mozart
(1756–1791)

original key:_____

**clarinet in B♭**

original key:_____

**French horn in F**

transposed key:_____

**clarinet in A**

transposed key:_____

# TRANSPOSITION FOR ORCHESTRAL INSTRUMENTS

2. The following excerpt is written for trumpet in B flat. Rewrite it at concert pitch. Name the original key and the new key.

Wolfgang Amadeus Mozart
(1756–1791)

original key:_____

transposed key:_____

3. The following excerpt is written for clarinet in A. Rewrite it at concert pitch. Name the original key and the new key.

Ludwig van Beethoven
(1770–1827)

original key:_____

transposed key:_____

4. The following excerpt is written for French horn in F. Rewrite it at concert pitch. Name the original key and the new key.

Ludwig van Beethoven
(1770–1827)

original key:_____

transposed key:_____

# SHORT SCORE AND OPEN SCORE

**Short Score**

This passage is written in **short** or **close** score:

Notice that:

1.  The music is written for four voices: soprano, alto, tenor, and bass (SATB).
2.  The treble staff is shared by the soprano (S) and alto (A). The bass staff is shared by the tenor (T) and bass (B).
3.  The stems for the soprano and tenor go up, and the stems for the alto and bass go down.

**Open Score**

When music is written in **open score,** each voice or instrument has its own staff.

We will learn about two types of open score:

> **modern vocal score**
> **string quartet score**

**Modern Vocal Score**

Here is the same passage written in **modern vocal score**.

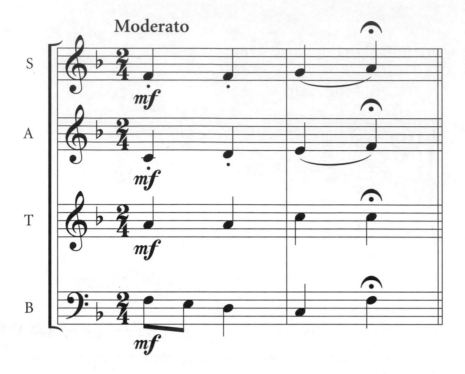

Note that:

1. The music is written for four voices: soprano, alto, tenor, and bass.

2. Each voice has its own staff and the parts line up vertically.

3. The alto part is written in the treble clef.

4. The tenor part is written in the treble clef, an octave higher than it sounds.
   In some publications, you may see a small "8" under the clef, which indicates that the notes should sound an octave lower than written.

5. The normal rules for stem direction apply.

6. The tempo marking is written only once (above the top staff), but dynamic markings are repeated for each part.

**String Quartet Score**

Here is the same passage written in **string quartet score**.

String quartet score is an instrumental score, rather than a vocal score. It is written for four string instruments.

1.   The top two staves, for the first and second violins (Vl. I and Vl. II), are written in the treble clef.

2.   The third staff, for the viola (Vla.), is written in the alto clef.

3.   The fourth staff, for the cello, (Vc.), is written in the bass clef.

4.   The normal rules for stem direction are followed.

5.   The tempo marking is written once, but dynamic markings are repeated for each part.

1. Transcribe the following Bach chorale excerpt into modern vocal score.

## Die Nacht ist kommen
### BWV 296

Johann Sebastian Bach
(1685–1750)

2. Transcribe the following excerpt into modern vocal score.

## Melody from Die Meistersinger von Nürnberg

3.  Transcribe the following excerpt into string quartet score.

## Magdalena
### op. 22, no. 6

Johannes Brahms
(1833–1897)

Source: *Marienlieder*, op. 22 (1859)

4.  Transcribe the following excerpt into short score.

## The Heavens Are Telling

Franz Joseph Haydn
(1732–1804)

Source: *The Creation*

5.   Transcribe the following excerpt into short score.

## Christ lag in Todesbanden
### BWV 279

Johann Sebastian Bach
(1685–1750)

# MELODY WRITING

Melodies contain three types of movement:

1. Movement by step. This is often called *conjunct* movement.

Hungarian Folk melody

2. Movement by leap. This is often called *disjunct* movement.

Jules Massenet
(1842–1912)

3. Repetition of a note before movement.

Nursery tune

Most melodies consist of a combination of these three types of movement. A melody should have a sense of shape or direction. Often a melody rises to a high point (or climax) and then moves down again. Motion by step is most common. Leaps add interest and contrast, but too many leaps may cause a melody to lose its shape.

A melody has two main elements:

1.  The **melodic structure**—the general shape or curve of the melody.

2.  The **rhythmic structure**—the rhythmic pattern that unifies the melody.

These two elements combine to form a melody.

English dance

Here are some important points to remember when you write a melody:

1.  Make sure the melody ends in a way that feels complete. One way to achieve this is to end your melody on the tonic.

2.  Remember that the shape of the melody is important. Your melody should have a sense of direction. For example, it might move to a high point and then down again. Try not to shift aimlessly around the same few notes.

3.  For the most part, use stepwise or scale-like movement. Add some leaps for contrast, but don't use too many or the melody may lose its shape.

4.  Avoid leaps of an augmented interval between melody notes (especially augmented 2nds and 4ths). If your melody is in a minor key, it is best to use the melodic form of the scale.

5.  Try to develop the ability to hear in your mind what you write down on paper. Use your imagination to improve the quality of your melodies. Try out your melodies by playing them and experimenting with different patterns.

Here are some strong ending patterns for melodies. The numbers indicate scale degrees.

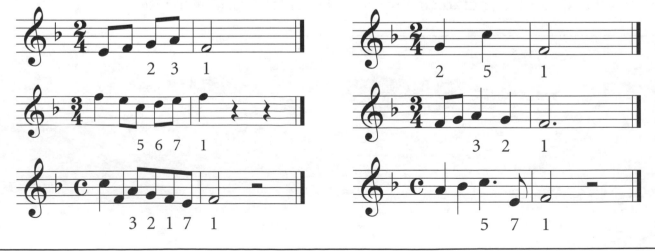

1. Write melodies in the following keys using these rhythmic patterns. (The first two measures of the first melody have been given as an example.) When you finish each melody, try singing it.

(a) G major

(b) B♭ major

(c) A minor

(d) F major

(e) E minor

**Writing a Response to a Given Melody**

Melodies often have a "question and answer" form: the first phrase (the question) is followed by a second phrase (the answer) that responds to the first phrase. Often the first phrase of a question-and-answer melody ends with an imperfect cadence, and the second phrase ends with a perfect cadence.

Here are several techniques or methods for writing the responding phrase of a question-and-answer melody.

**Method 1: Repeat the opening phrase.**

In the melody below, the first phrase (the question) ends with an imperfect cadence, but the second phrase (the answer) ends with a perfect cadence. To do this, the composer repeats the melody of the first phase, but changes the ending so that it fits the notes needed for a perfect cadence.

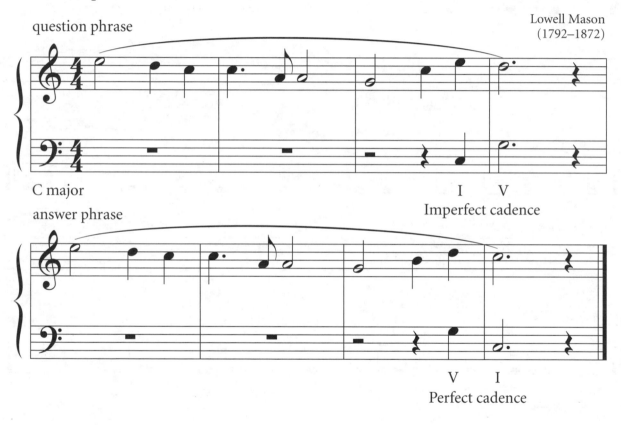

The easiest way to make sure you can end your melody with a perfect cadence is to end the melody on the tonic. The best way to approach the tonic note is from either the supertonic or the leading note.

1. Name the key of the following melody. Write a responding phrase using "Method 1." Write cadences at the end of each phrase, identify the chords, and name the cadences.

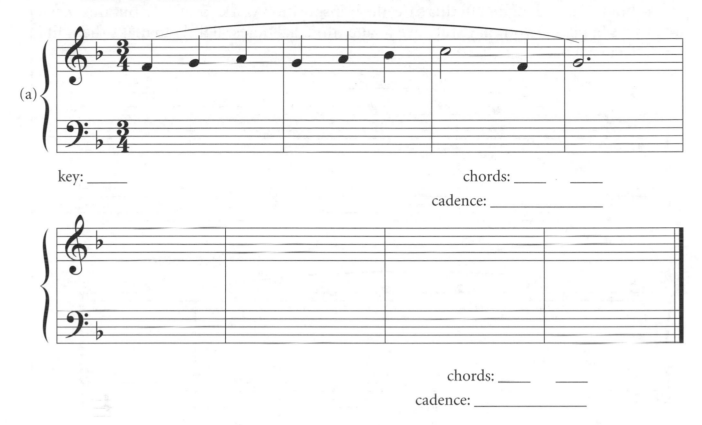

(a)

key: _____    chords: _____ . _____

cadence: _____

chords: _____    _____

cadence: _____

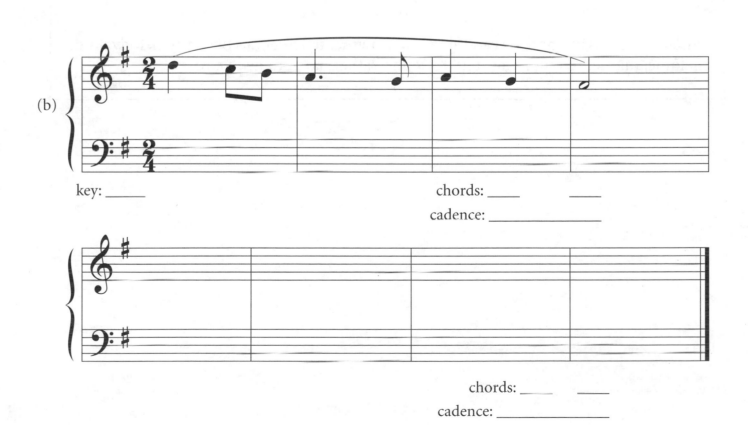

(b)

key: _____    chords: _____    _____

cadence: _____

chords: _____    _____

cadence: _____

**Method 2: Repeat the opening phrase a 2nd higher or a 2nd lower.**

In the example below, the second phrase (the answer) has the same shape as the first phrase but it is a 2nd higher. In this case, the transposition works perfectly, but this may not always happen—you may still have to alter the final notes slightly to make them fit the perfect cadence.

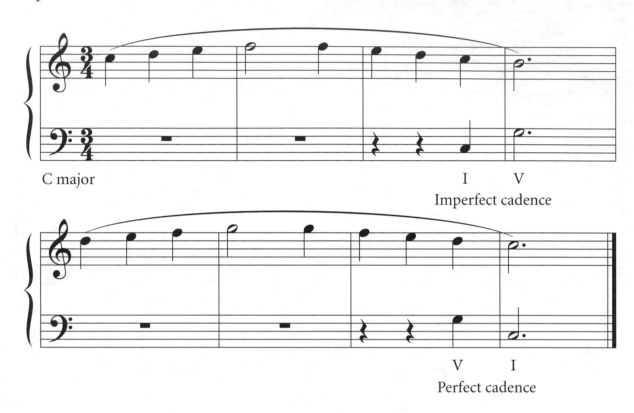

C major

I   V

Imperfect cadence

V   I

Perfect cadence

When using this method, be careful to avoid augmented intervals between melody notes; melodic augmented intervals tend to sound rather harsh or awkward.

2. Name the key of the following melody. Write a responding phrase using "Method 2." Write cadences at the end of each phrase, identify the chords, and name the cadences.

(a)

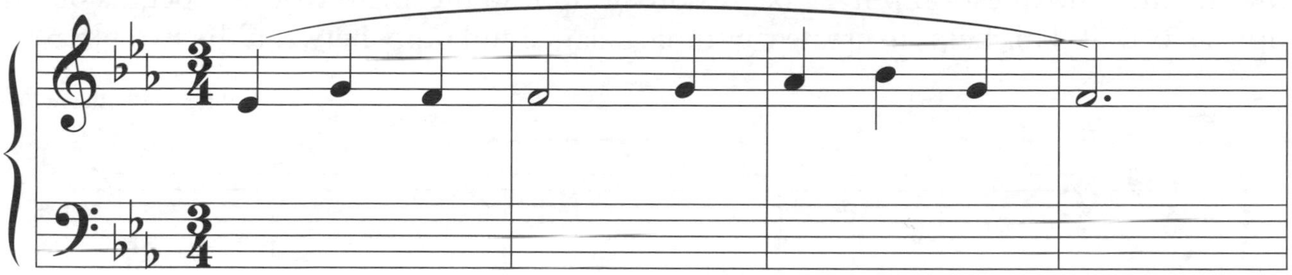

key: _____

chords: _____ _____

cadence: _____

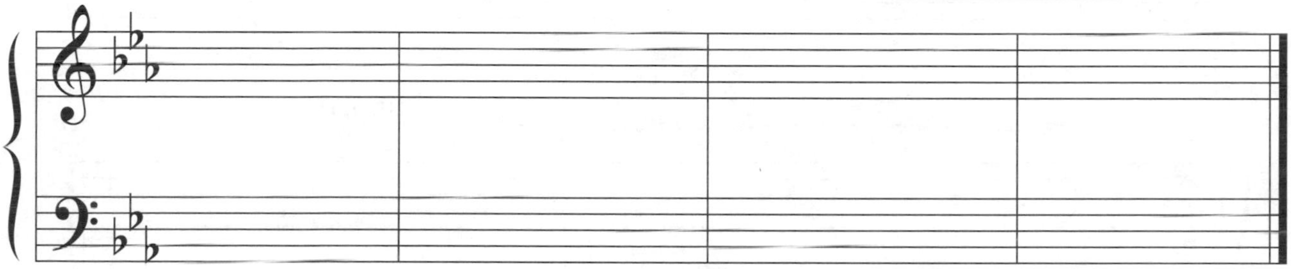

chords: _____ _____

cadence: _____

(b)

key: _____

chords: _____ _____

cadence: _____

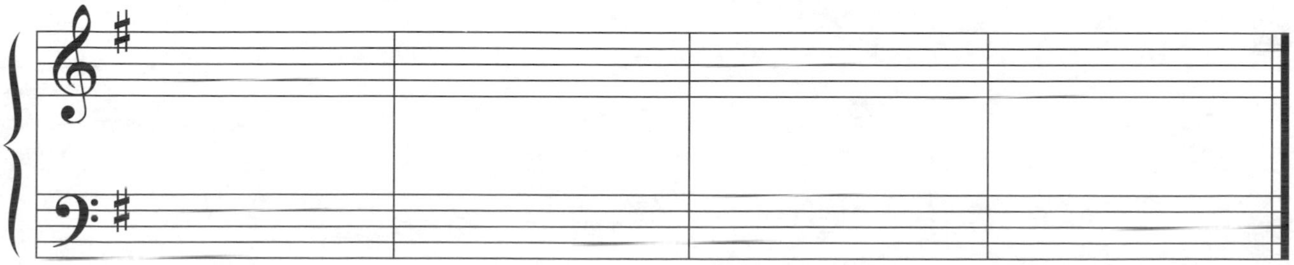

chords: _____ _____

cadence: _____

**Method 3: Repeat the opening phrase a 5th higher or a 4th lower.**

In the example below, the second phrase (the answer) has been changed to accommodate a perfect cadence. The second phrase has the same shape as the first phrase but it is a 4th lower. Since the question phrase begins on an upbeat, the answer phrase begins on an upbeat as well. This helps to create rhythmic balance and unity between the two phrases.

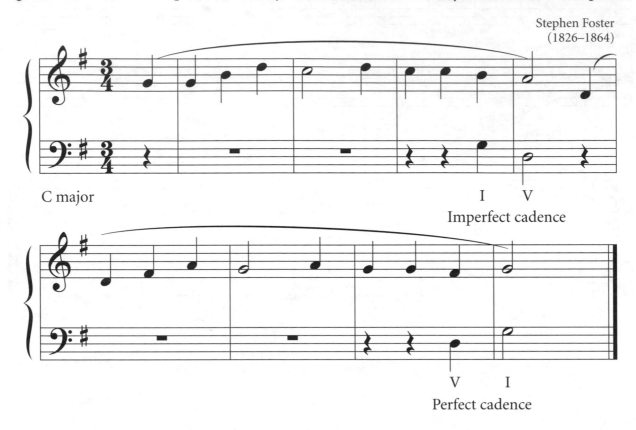

Stephen Foster
(1826–1864)

C major

I   V

Imperfect cadence

V   I

Perfect cadence

Always remember to check your response melody for augmented intervals, and adjust the notes if necessary to avoid these intervals.

3.  Name the key of the following melody. Write a responding phrase using "Method 3." Write cadences at the end of each phrase, identify the chords, and name the cadences.

(a)

key: _____          chords: _____     _____
                      cadence: _____

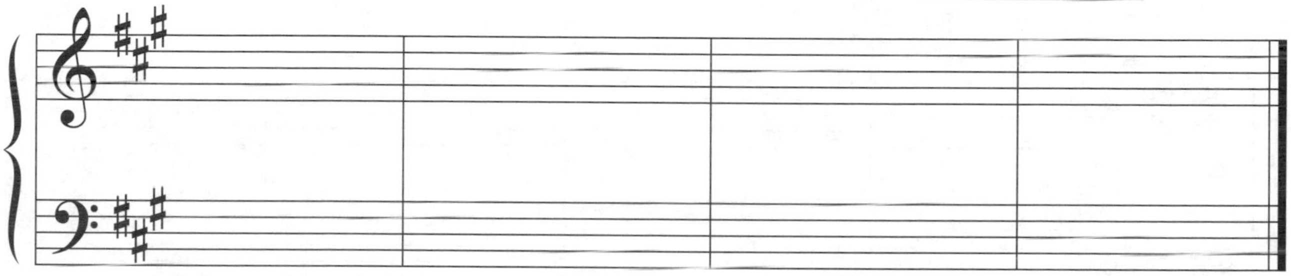

          chords: _____     _____
          cadence: _____

(b)

key: _____          chords: _____     _____
                      cadence: _____

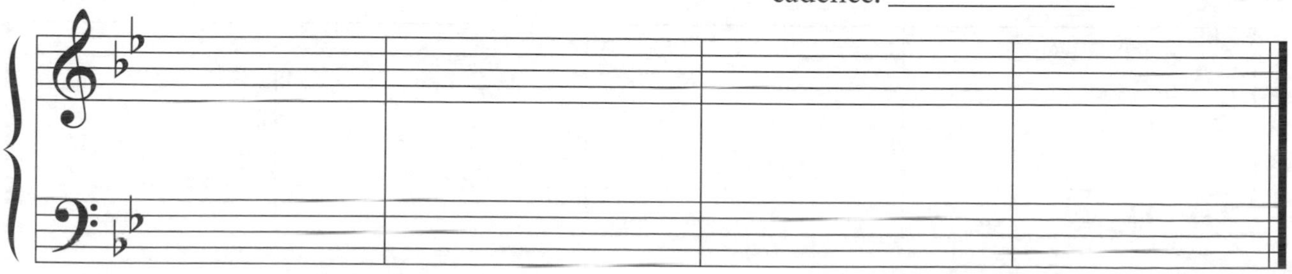

          chords: _____     _____
          cadence: _____

## MELODY WRITING

4. Name the keys of the following melodies. Write a responding phrase to each one. Write cadences at the end of each phrase, identify the chords, and name the cadences.

Stephen Foster
(1826–1864)

(a)

key: _____     chords: _____  _____

cadence: _____

chords: _____  _____

cadence: _____

(b)

key: _____     chords: _____  _____

cadence: _____

chords: _____  _____

cadence: _____

# MUSIC ANALYSIS

**B**
**I**
**A**

1. Analyze the following music by answering the questions below.

## Study in C

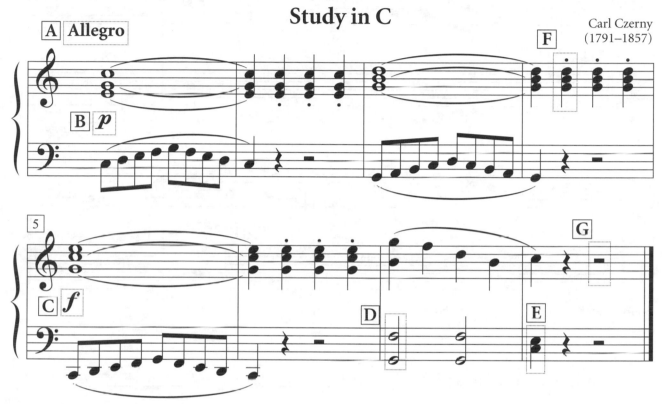

Source: *First Instruction in Piano Playing: 100 Recreations,* no. 28

(a) What is the title of this piece? _____

(b) Name the composer of this piece: _____

(c) Add the time signature to the music.

(d) Define the term at A : _____

(e) Explain the sign at B : _____

(f) Explain the sign at C : _____

(g) Name the intervals at D : _____ E :_____

(h) Name the triad at F : _____

(i) Explain the sign at G : _____

(j) Name the highest note: _____ Name the lowest note: _____

# Music Analysis

B I A

2.  Analyze the following music by answering the questions below.

## Carefree

Daniel Gottlob Türk
(1750–1813)

Source: *120 Pieces for Aspring Players,* book 1, no. 4

(a)  What is the title of this piece? _____

(b)  Name the composer of this piece: _____

(c)  Add the time signature to the music.

(d)  How many measures are there in this piece?_____

(e)  Define the word at A : _____

(f)  Explain the sign at B : _____

(g)  Explain the sign at C : _____

(h)  Name the intervals at D : _____  E : _____  F : _____

3. Analyze the following music by answering the questions below.

## Waltz*

Carl Czerny
(1791–1857)

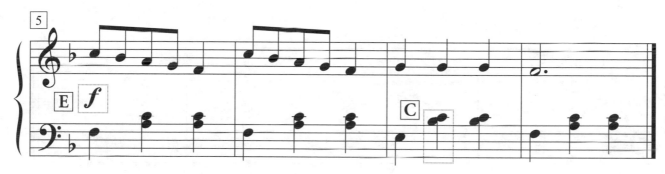

\* Transposed from original key of C major.
Source: *Five Finger Studies for Piano Solo,* op. 777, no. 3

(a) Add the time signature to the music.

(b) What is the title of this excerpt? _____

(c) Name the composer of this excerpt: _____

(d) Name the key of this excerpt: _____

(e) How many measures are there in this excerpt? _____

(f) Name the intervals at A : _____ B : _____ C : _____

(g) Explain the sign at D : _____

(h) Explain the sign at E : _____

## MUSIC ANALYSIS

**I**
**A**

4. Analyze the following music by answering the questions below.

### Allegretto

Antonio Diabelli
(1781–1858)

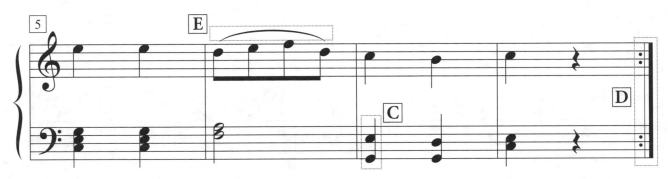

(a) Define *allegretto*: _____

(b) Add the correct time signature to the music.

(c) Name the composer of this excerpt: _____

(d) For the chord at [A], name the root: _____ type: _____ position: _____

(e) Name the intervals at [B]: _____ [C]: _____

(f) Explain the sign at [D]: _____

(g) Explain the sign at [E]: _____

(h) Name the key of this excerpt: _____

(i) How many measures are there in this excerpt? _____

**I**
**A**

5. Analyze the following music by answering the questions below.

## Sonatina
### Anh. 5/1

Ludwig van Beethoven
(1770–1827)

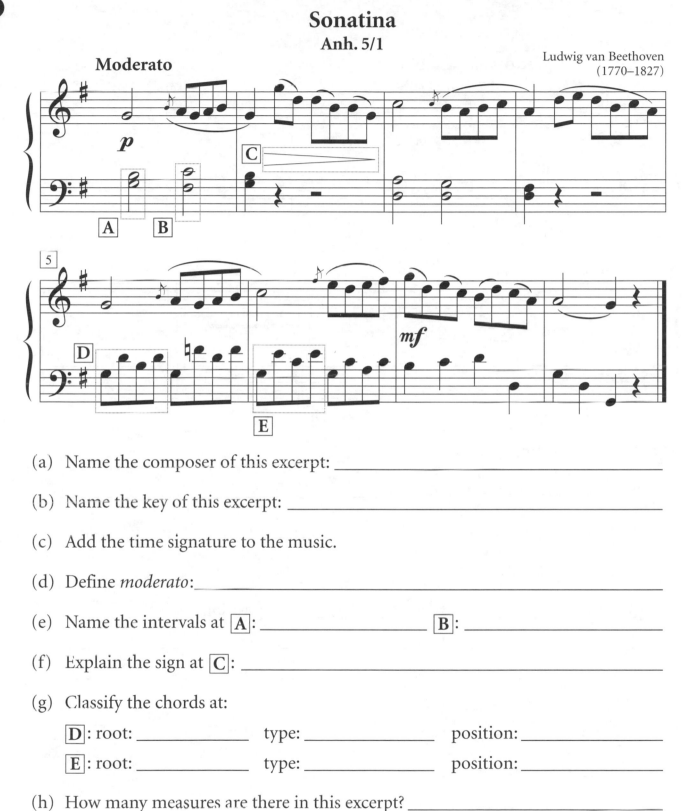

(a) Name the composer of this excerpt: _____

(b) Name the key of this excerpt: _____

(c) Add the time signature to the music.

(d) Define *moderato*: _____

(e) Name the intervals at ⟮A⟯: _____ ⟮B⟯: _____

(f) Explain the sign at ⟮C⟯: _____

(g) Classify the chords at:

⟮D⟯: root: _____ type: _____ position: _____

⟮E⟯: root: _____ type: _____ position: _____

(h) How many measures are there in this excerpt? _____

## Music Analysis

**I**
**A**

6. Analyze the following music by answering the questions below.

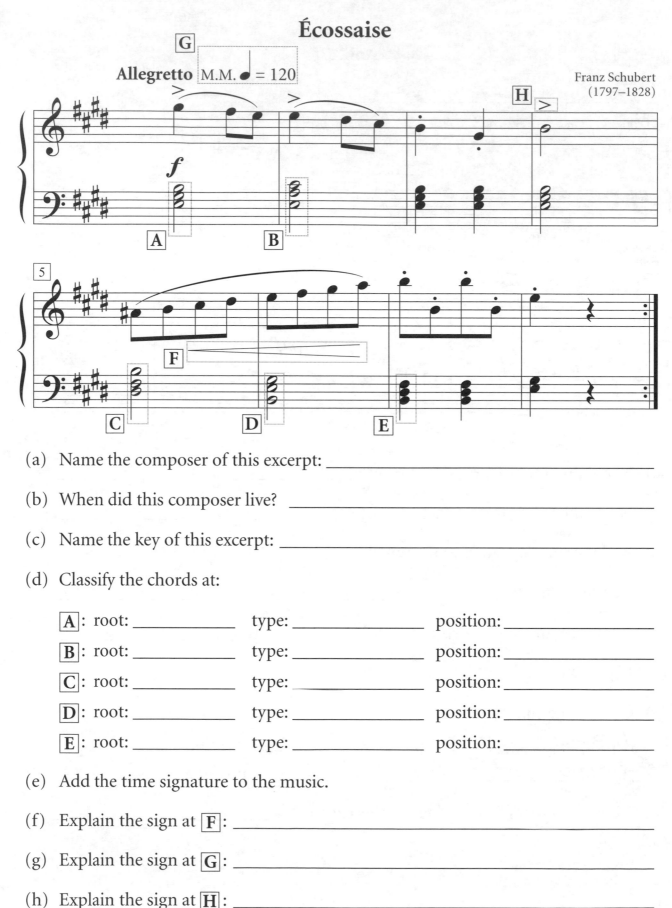

(a) Name the composer of this excerpt: _____

(b) When did this composer live? _____

(c) Name the key of this excerpt: _____

(d) Classify the chords at:

    A: root: _____    type: _____    position: _____

    B: root: _____    type: _____    position: _____

    C: root: _____    type: _____    position: _____

    D: root: _____    type: _____    position: _____

    E: root: _____    type: _____    position: _____

(e) Add the time signature to the music.

(f) Explain the sign at F: _____

(g) Explain the sign at G: _____

(h) Explain the sign at H: _____

## Motives

A **motive** is a short melodic or rhythmic idea. Motives consist of two or more notes and can be found in almost all musical compositions. Composers often expand or develop these motives to create a piece of music. The following, one of music's most well-known motives, is taken from Beethoven's Symphony No. 5. Most of this symphony is based on the four-note motive seen below. This motive is rhythmic, as well as melodic. It consists of three repeated eighth notes followed by a half note a 3rd below.

### Symphony no. 5 (1st movement)

Ludwig van Beethoven
(1770–1827)

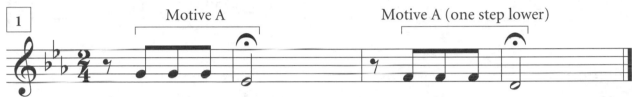

The example below, taken from the same symphony, illustrates an alteration of motive A. Here, the rhythm is the same but the intervals change. After the eighth notes, the melody leaps down a 5th instead of a 3rd and continues the half-note motion found at the end of the motive. This example is from measure 59 in the first movement. Often in music scores, the measure numbers are identified for you. When you refer to a measure number you use the abbreviation m. for one measure (m. 59), and the abbreviation mm. for more than one measure (mm. 59–62).

### Symphony no. 5 (1st movement)

Ludwig van Beethoven
(1770–1827)

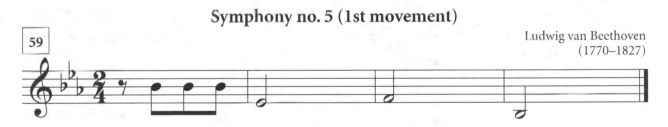

Study Beethoven's treatment of the same motive used in mm. 19–26 in the 3rd movement. Notice the changes in time signature, note values, and intervals. Although they are different, the real essence of the motive remains intact.

### Symphony no. 5 (3rd movement)

Ludwig van Beethoven
(1770–1827)

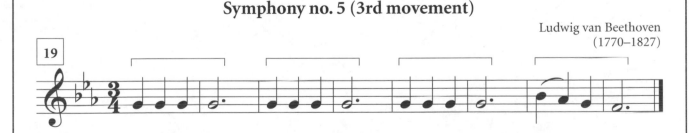

## Sequence

A **sequence** is an exact repetition of a passage at a lower or higher pitch. If the repetition is of a melody, it is a **melodic sequence.** If the repetition is a series of chords, it is a **harmonic sequence.** The example below illustrates a sequence. Beethoven uses material from motive A and repeats it stepping up a semitone with each statement.

### Symphony no. 5 (1st movement)

Ludwig van Beethoven
(1770–1827)

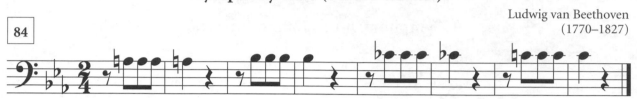

## Imitation

Many compositions contain a melodic or rhythmic device called **imitation.** Imitation is the repetition of a motive or a complete musical idea or phrase in another voice or clef. Study the following Bach *Invention.* This piece is based on a melody consisting of two motives. Motive A is based on eighth notes, and motive B is based on sixteenth notes. The melody starts in the treble clef and before it is complete, the bass imitates it by stating the very same melody, one measure later and one octave lower.

### Invention no. 8

Johann Sebastian Bach
(1685–1750)

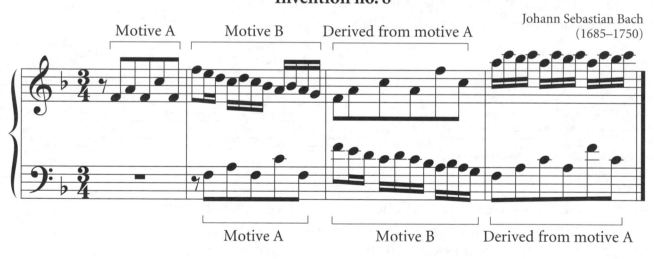

### Inversion

**Inversion** means to turn something upside down. We have studied interval inversion, but here inversion applies not just to one interval, but to a motive or an entire melody. Study the example below observing how the composer inverts the opening motive in the second phrase. Unlike interval inversion, motivic or melodic inversion is not always exact. Here the composer alters the intervals so that they continue to outline the C major chord. Melodic inversion may use exact intervals, but many times, as in the example below, it is about the shape of the melody.

## Sonatina in C
### op. 36, no. 1 (1st movement)

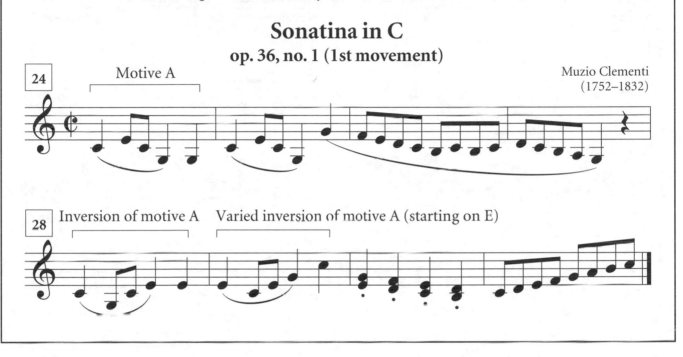

## MUSIC ANALYSIS

**A** 7. Analyze the following music by answering the questions below.

### Sonata
#### Hob. XVI:37, III

(a) Add the correct time signature directly on the music.

(b) What is the final measure number of this excerpt? _____

(c) Name the key of this excerpt: _____

(d) Name the composer of this excerpt: _____

(e) When did the composer live? _____

(f) Find one example of a **sequence** and mark it directly on the score.

(g) Find one example of **inversion** and mark it directly on the score.

(f) Name the intervals at **A**: _____ **B**: _____ **C**: _____

(i) Define *presto ma non troppo*:_____

**A** 8. Analyze the following music by answering the questions below.

## Sonata
### Hob. XVI:37, I

Joseph Haydn
(1732–1809)

(a) Add the correct time signature directly on the music.

(b) How many measures are in this excerpt? _____

(c) Name the key of this excerpt: _____

(d) What is the title of this excerpt? _____

(e) Find one example of a **tritone** and mark it directly on the score.

(f) Find one example of a **slur** and mark it directly on the score.

(g) Name the intervals at A: _____ B: _____ C: _____

(h) Classify the chords at:

   D: root: _____ type: _____ position: _____
   E: root: _____ type: _____ position: _____
   F: root: _____ type: _____ position: _____

(i) Name and explain the sign at G: _____

## MUSIC ANALYSIS

**A**　9.　Analyze the following music by answering the questions below.

# L'Arabesque

Friedrich Johann Franz Burgmüller
(1806–1874)

Source: *25 Études progessives*, op. 100, no. 2

(a)　Add the correct time signature to the music.

(b)　Name the composer of this excerpt: _____

(c)　How many measures are there in this excerpt? _____

(d)　Define *allegro scherzando*: _____

(e)　Define *leggiero*: _____

(f)　Classify the chords at:

　　　**A**: root: _____　type: _____　position: _____

　　　**B**: root: _____　type: _____　position: _____

　　　**C**: root: _____　type: _____　position: _____

　　　**D**: root: _____　type: _____　position: _____

(g)　Explain the sign at **E**: _____

(h)　Find an example of a **sequence** and mark it directly on the score.

　*THE COMPLETE ELEMENTARY MUSIC RUDIMENTS*

# PRACTICE TESTS

**B**
**I**
**A**

**PRACTICE TEST 1**

1.  Name the following notes.

2.  Write the following notes.

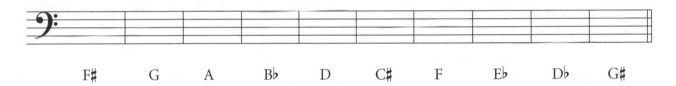

F♯    G    A    B♭    D    C♯    F    E♭    D♭    G♯

3.  Write the following scales, ascending and descending, in the treble clef.

    (a)    D harmonic minor, using a key signature
    (b)    A major, using accidentals instead of a key signature
    (c)    The relative minor of A major, melodic form, using a key signature

(a)

(b)

(c)

4.  Name the following intervals.

5. Mark the following as chromatic semitones (CS), diatonic semitones (DS), or whole tones (WT).

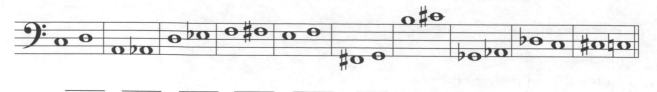

_____ _____ _____ _____

6. Add time signatures to the following one-measure rhythms.

7. Complete the following measures by adding rests under the brackets.

8. Write the following broken triads, using a key signature for each.
   (a)    the tonic triad of E♭ major
   (b)    the dominant triad of C♯ minor
   (c)    the subdominant triad of A major
   (d)    the dominant triad of E minor
   (e)    the subdominant triad of G minor

   (a)              (b)              (c)              (d)              (e)

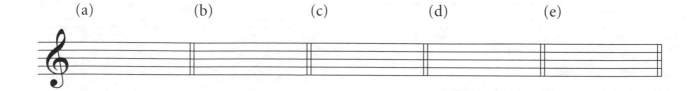

9. Write the following notes, using a key signature for each.

   (a)   the tonic of D major
   (b)   the subdominant of F minor
   (c)   the dominant of E major
   (d)   the tonic of D minor
   (c)   the subdominant of C major

10. Name the key of the following melody. Transpose it up one octave into the treble clef.

key: _____

10

11. Analyze the following music by answering the questions below.

## Minuet in C
### K 6

(a) Add the correct time signature directly on the music.

(b) Name the composer of this excerpt: _____

(c) When did the composer live? _____

(d) Name the highest note in this excerpt: _____

(e) Name the intervals at [A]: _____ [B]: _____

(f) Name the sign at [C]: _____

(g) How many measures are in this excerpt? _____

(f) How many accidentals are in this excerpt? _____

(i) Define *allegretto:* _____

100

**PRACTICE TEST 2**

1. Name the following intervals.

$\dfrac{}{5}$

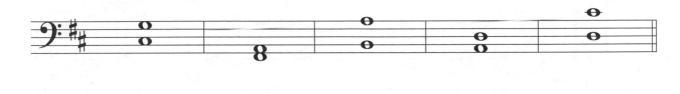

———  ———  ———  ———  ———

$\dfrac{}{5}$ 2. Invert the intervals above and name the inversions.

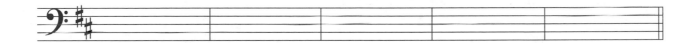

$\dfrac{}{10}$ 3. Write the following triads, using a key signature for each.
   (a)   the tonic triad of B♭ major
   (b)   the dominant triad of C♯ minor
   (c)   the subdominant triad of D♭ major
   (d)   the supertonic triad of F♯ major
   (e)   the mediant triad of A♭ minor

(a)                (b)                (c)                (d)                (e)

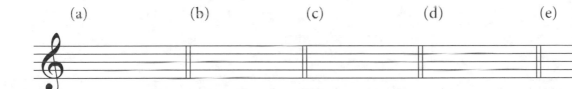

$\dfrac{}{10}$ 4. Name each of the following scales as major, natural minor, harmonic minor, melodic minor, whole-tone, major pentatonic, minor pentatonic, blues, chromatic, or octatonic.

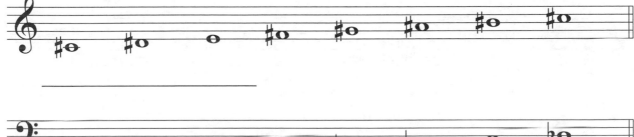

———————————————

———————————————

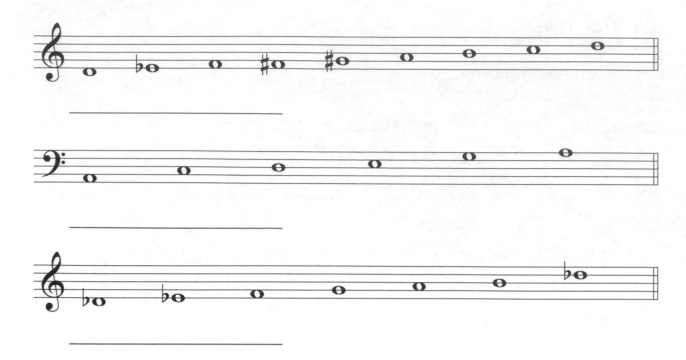

_____

_____

_____

5. Name the key of the following melody. Transpose it up a minor 6th, and name the new key.

Franz Schubert
(1797–1828)

key: _____

key: _____

6. Add rests under the brackets to complete the following one-measure rhythms.

___
10

7.   Add time signatures to the following one-measure rhythms.

___
10

8.   Name the keys of the following musical fragments. Write the chord symbols at the end of each and name the cadence as perfect, plagal, or imperfect.

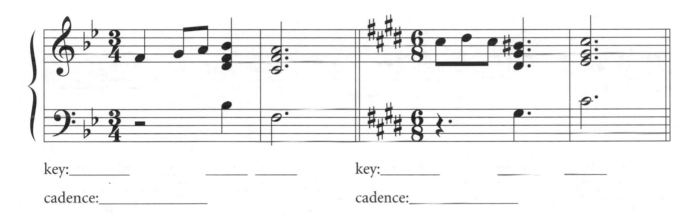

key:_____          _____   _____          key:_____          ___   _____

cadence:_____                       cadence:_____

___
10

9.   (a)   Name the minor key for each key signature.
     (b)   Name the degree of the scale for each note.

(a)_____    _____          _____    _____    _____

(b)_____    _____          _____    _____    _____

10

10. Rewrite the following melodies, omitting the accidentals and using key signatures. Name the key of each melody.

key: _____

key: _____

10

11. Analyze the following piece of music by answering the questions below.

# Pièces de clavecin
## op. 1

Joseph-Hector Fiocco
(1703–1741)

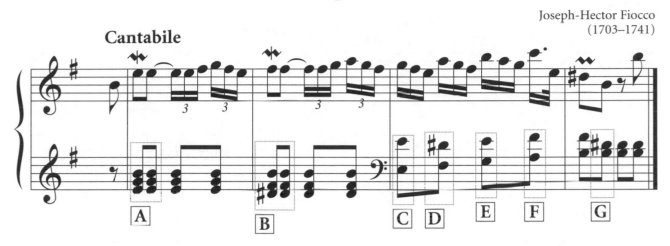

(a) Add the correct time signature directly on the music.

(b) Name the composer of this excerpt: _____

(c) Name the key of this excerpt: _____

(d) Classify the chords at:

A: root: _____  type: _____  position: _____

B: root: _____  type: _____  position: _____

(e) Name the intervals at C: _____  D: _____

E: _____  F: _____  G: _____

(f) Define *cantabile:* _____

100

# Practice Tests

## A   Practice Test 3

$\dfrac{}{10}$   1.   Add the proper clef, key signature, and accidentals to form the following scales.

D♭ major

G♯ minor harmonic

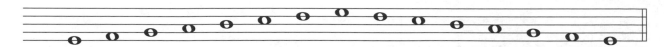

F minor melodic

Dorian mode starting on C

Lydian mode starting on G

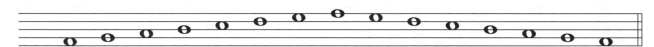

$\dfrac{}{10}$   2.   Write the following chords, using key signatures:

    (a)     root position dominant triad in D minor in the bass clef
    (b)     first inversion leading-note triad in F♯ major in the treble clef
    (c)     second inversion supertonic triad in B♭ minor in the alto clef
    (d)     third inversion dominant 7th chord in F major in the bass clef
    (e)     root position diminished 7th chord in E minor in the treble clef

    (a)                (b)            (c)            (d)            (e)

3. For each of the following dominant 7th chords, name:
   (a)  the key to which it belongs
   (b)  the position

10

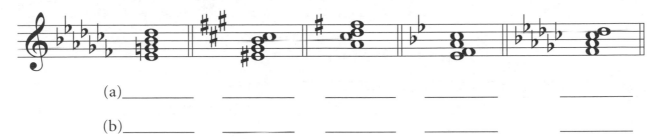

(a)_____   _____   _____   _____   _____

(b)_____   _____   _____   _____   _____

4. (a) Name the following intervals.

10

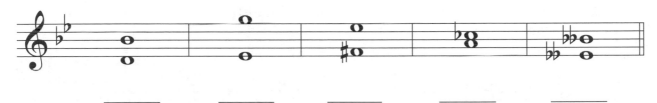

_____   _____   _____   _____   _____

(b) Invert the intervals above and name the inversions.

_____   _____   _____   _____   _____

5. Name the key of the following melody. Transpose it down a minor 3rd. Name the new key.

10

key: _____

key: _____

__10__    6.   Add rests under the brackets to complete the following one-measure rhythms.

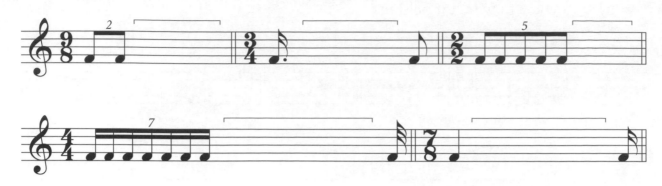

__10__    7.   For the following melodic fragments, name the key and write an appropriate
               cadence at the end. Symbolize the chords and identify the cadences as perfect,
               plagal, or imperfect.

key:_____          _____  _____          key:_____          _____  _____

cadence:_____                        cadence:_____

8. Transcribe the following passage in open score using string quartet score.

Johann Sebastian Bach
(1685–1750)

9. Add time signatures to the following rhythms.

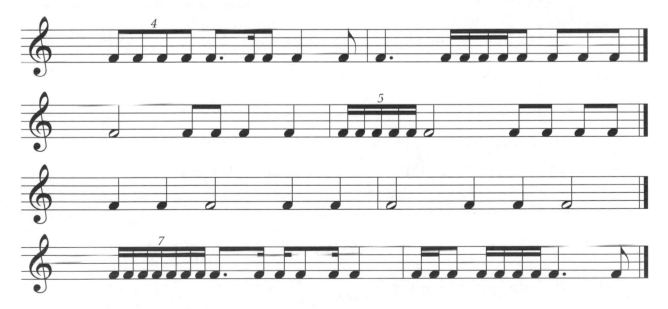

10. Analyze the following piece of music by answering the questions below.

## Sonatina
### op. 55, no. 4 (2nd movement)

Friedrich Kuhlau
(1786–1832)

**Andante con espressione**

(a)  Write the time signature directly on the music.

(b)  Name the composer of this excerpt: _____

(c)  Name the key of this excerpt: _____

(d)  Classify the chords at:

   A : root: _____   type: _____   position: _____
   B : root: _____   type: _____   position: _____
   C : root: _____   type: _____   position: _____

(e)  Name the intervals at D : _____   E : _____

(f)  Circle and label one harmonic minor 6th in this excerpt.

(g)  Define *andante con espressione*.

_____

# TERMS AND SIGNS FOR EXAMINATIONS

| | | |
|---|---|---|
| ♩ | *a tempo* | return to the original tempo |
| ♪ | *accelerando, accel.* | becoming quicker |
| ⁓ | accent ♩ | stressed note or chord |
| ✓ | *adagio* | a slow tempo (between *andante* and *largo*) |
| | *ad libitum, ad lib.* | at the liberty of the performer |
| | *agitato* | agitated |
| | *alla, all'* | in the manner of |
| | *allargando, allarg.* | broadening, becoming slower |
| | *allegretto* | fairly fast (a little slower than *allegro*) |
| | *allegro* | fast |
| | *andante* | moderately slow; at a walking pace |
| | *andantino* | a little faster than *andante* |
| | *animato* | lively, animated |
| | *arco* | for stringed instruments: resume bowing after a *pizzicato* passage |
| | *assai* | much, very much (for example, *allegro assai*: very fast) |
| | *attacca* | proceed without a break |
| | *ben, bene* | well (for example, *ben marcato*: well marked) |
| | *bewegt* | agitated, excited |
| | *brillante* | brilliant |
| | *calando* | becoming slower and softer |
| ⁓ | *cantabile* | in a singing style |
| | *cédez* | yield; hold the tempo back |
| | cluster | chord consisting of a combination of at least three adjacent notes of any scale |
| | *col, coll', colla, colle* | with (for example, *coll'ottava*: with an added octave) |
| | *comodo, commodo* | at a comfortable, easy tempo |
| | *con* | with |
| | *con brio* | with vigor or spirit |
| | *con espressione* | with expression |
| | *con fuoco* | with fire |
| | *con grazia* | with grace |
| | *con moto* | with movement |
| | *con pedale, con ped.* | with pedal |
| | *con sordino* | with mute |
| | *crescendo, cresc.* | becoming louder |
| ⁓ | *da capo, D.C.* | from the beginning |
| ⁓ | *dal segno, D.S. al* 𝄋 | from the sign |

# Terms and Signs for Examinations

| | |
|---|---|
| *D.C. al Fine* | repeat from the beginning and end at *Fine* |
| *decrescendo, decresc.* ⟍ | becoming softer |
| *diminuendo, dim.* | becoming softer |
| *dolce* | sweet |
| *dolente* | sad |
| | |
| *e, ed* | and |
| *espressivo* | expression, with expression |
| | |
| *fermata,* ⌢ | pause; hold note or rest longer than written value |
| ✓ *fine* | the end |
| *forte,* ***f*** | loud |
| *fortepiano,* ***fp*** | loud, then suddenly soft |
| *fortissimo,* ***ff*** | very loud |
| | |
| *giocoso* | humorous, joyful |
| *grandioso* | grand, grandiose |
| *grave* | slow and solemn |
| *grazioso* | graceful |
| | |
| *langsam* | slow |
| *largamente* | broadly |
| *larghetto* | not as slow as *largo* |
| *largo* | very slow and broad |
| *legato* | smooth |
| *léger* | light, lightly |
| *leggiero* | light, nimble, quick |
| *lentement* | slowly |
| *lento* | slow |
| *l'istesso tempo* | the same tempo |
| *loco* | return to normal register |
| | |
| *ma* | but (for example, *ma non troppo*: but not too much) |
| *maestoso* | majestic |
| *mano destra, M.D.* | right hand |
| *mano sinistra, M.S.* | left hand |
| *marcato, marc.* | marked or stressed |
| *martellato* | strongly accented, hammered |
| *mässig* | moderate, moderately |
| *meno* | less |
| *meno mosso* | less movement, slower |
| *mesto* | sad, mournful |
| *mezzo forte,* ***mf*** | moderately loud |
| *mezzo piano,* ***mp*** | moderately soft |
| *mit* | with |

*The Complete Elementary Music Rudiments*

| | |
|---|---|
| *mit Ausdruck* | with expression |
| M.M. | metronome marking (Maelzel's Metronome) |
| *moderato* | at a moderate tempo |
| *modéré* | at a moderate tempo |
| *molto* | much, very |
| *morendo* | dying, fading away |
| *mouvement* | tempo, motion |
| | |
| *non* | not |
| *non troppo* | not too much |
| | |
| *ottava, 8va* | the interval of an octave |
| *8va- - - -* ¬ | play one octave above the written pitch |
| *8va- - - -* ⌟ | play one octave below the written pitch |
| *pedale, ped.* 𝄢. |⎯⎯⎯⎯| | pedal |
| *pesante* | weighty, with emphasis |
| *pianissimo,* **pp** | very soft |
| *piano,* **p** | soft |
| *più* | more |
| *più mosso* | more movement, quicker |
| *pizzicato* | for stringed instruments: pluck the string instead of bowing |
| *poco* | little |
| *poco a poco* | little by little |
| polychord | combination of two or more different chords |
| *prestissimo* | as fast as possible |
| *presto* | very fast |
| *prima, primo* | first; the upper part of a duet |
| *prima volta* | first time |
| | |
| quartal chord | chord built on a series of 4ths |
| *quasi* | almost, as if |
| *quindicesima alta, 15ma* | two octaves higher |
| | |
| *rallentando, rall.* | slowing down |
| repeat signs 𝄆 𝄇 | repeat the music between the signs |
| *risoluto* | resolute |
| *ritardando, rit.* | slowing down gradually |
| *ritenuto, riten.* | suddenly slower, held back |
| *rubato* | a flexible tempo using slight variations of speed to enhance musical expression |
| | |
| *scherzando* | playful |
| *schnell* | fast |
| *seconda, secondo* | second; the lower part of a duet |

# TERMS AND SIGNS FOR EXAMINATIONS

| | |
|---|---|
| *seconda volta* | second time |
| *sehr* | very |
| *semplice* | simple |
| *sempre* | always, continuously |
| *senza* | without |
| seventh (7th) chords | chords consisting of a root, third, fifth, and seventh |
| *sforzando, sf, sfz* | a sudden strong accent of a single note or chord |
| *simile* | continue in the same manner as indicated |
| slur | play the notes *legato* |
| *sonore* | sonorous |
| *sopra* | above |
| *sostenuto* | sustained |
| *sotto voce* | softly, subdued, under the breath |
| *spiritoso* | spirited |
| *staccato* | detached |
| *stringendo* | pressing, becoming faster |
| *subito* | suddenly |
| | |
| *tacet* | be silent |
| *tempo* | speed at which music is performed |
| *Tempo primo, Tempo I* | return to the original tempo |
| *tenuto* | held, sustained |
| tie | hold for the combined value of the notes |
| *tranquillo* | quiet, tranquil |
| *tre corde* | three strings: release the left piano pedal |
| triad | chord consisting of a root, third, and fifth |
| *troppo* | too much |
| *tutti* | a passage for the entire ensemble |
| | |
| *una corda* | one string: depress the left piano pedal |
| | |
| *vite* | fast |
| *vivace* | lively, brisk |
| *vivo* | lively |
| *volta* | time |
| *volti subito, v.s.* | turn the page quickly |

# Glossary

| | |
|---|---|
| accidental | a symbol, placed in front of a note, that raises or lowers its pitch |
| *alla breve* ¢ | cut time, another name for the time signature $\frac{2}{2}$ |
| alto clef | a clef that indicates the location of middle C on the third line of the staff |
| augmented interval | an interval that is one chromatic semitone larger than the equivalent major or perfect interval |
| augmented triad | a three-note chord consisting of a major 3rd and an augmented 5th above the root |
| bar line | a vertical line that divides the staff into measures |
| bass clef 𝄢 | the clef that indicates the location of F on the fourth line of the staff |
| beam | a horizontal line that connects two or more eighth, sixteenth, or thirty-second notes |
| *breve* | double whole note: in $\frac{4}{2}$ time, a note equal to four beats |
| blues scale | a major scale in which the 3rd, the 7th, and sometimes the 5th degrees are lowered |
| C clef 𝄡 | a clef that indicates the location of middle C on a line of the staff |
| cadence | two chords or implied harmonies that end a phrase of music, creating a place of rest |
| chorale style | a style of written music for four distinct voices: soprano, alto, tenor, and bass (SATB) |
| chord | a combination of notes that are played together |
| chromatic scale | a scale made up only of semitones |
| chromatic semitone | a semitone that consists of two notes with the same letter name (for example, G–G♯) |
| circle of fifths | a diagram that shows how keys are related by perfect 5ths |
| clef | the sign placed at the beginning of a staff to indicate the location of notes |
| close position | a position of a chord in which the notes are as close together as possible |
| common time | another name for the time signature $\frac{4}{4}$ |
| compound duple time | time signatures that indicate two beats in each measure—for example, $\frac{6}{4}$, $\frac{6}{8}$, $\frac{6}{16}$ —where each beat is divisible by three |
| compound interval | an interval that is larger than an octave |
| compound quadruple time | time signatures that indicate four beats in each measure—for example, $\frac{12}{4}$, $\frac{12}{8}$, $\frac{12}{16}$ —where each beat is divisible by three |
| compound time | time signatures in which each beat is divisible by three |
| compound triple time | time signatures that indicate three beats in each measure—for example, $\frac{9}{4}$, $\frac{9}{8}$, $\frac{9}{16}$ —where each beat is divisible by three |
| cut time (*alla breve*) ¢ | another name for the time signature |
| diatonic semitone | a semitone that consists of two notes with different letter names (for example, G–A♭) |
| diminished interval | an interval that is one chromatic semitone smaller than the equivalent a minor or perfect interval |
| diminished triad | a three-note chord consisting of a minor 3rd and a diminished 5th above the root |

# GLOSSARY

| | |
|---|---|
| dominant 7th chord | a four-note chord consisting of a major dominant triad plus a minor 7th above the root |
| double flat ♭♭ | the sign that lowers the pitch of a note one whole tone |
| double sharp ✗ | the sign that raises the pitch of a note one whole tone |
| double whole note, breve ‖o‖ | in $\frac{4}{2}$ time, a note equal to four beats |
| duplet | in compound time, a group of two notes that are played in the time of three notes of the same value |
| enharmonic | describes notes of the same pitch that are named differently (for example, F♯ and G♭, or D♯ and E♭) |
| enharmonic change | a change of the name of a note without a change in pitch (for example, B♮ to C♭ |
| enharmonic equivalents | two notes that have the same pitch but different names |
| fifth | in a chord, the note that is the interval of a 5th above the root |
| first inversion | the position of a chord when the third is the lowest note |
| flag | a small curved line that, when attached to a note stem, indicates an eighth note (two flags indicate a sixteenth note; three indicate a thirty-second note) |
| flat ♭ | the sign that lowers the pitch of a note one semitone |
| grand staff | the combination of the treble and bass staves |
| harmonic interval | the distance between two notes played at the same time |
| harmonic minor scale | a scale formed by raising the seventh degree of the natural minor scale. There are semitones between notes $\hat{2}$ and $\hat{3}$, notes $\hat{5}$ and $\hat{6}$, and notes $\hat{7}$ and $\hat{8}(\hat{1})$. |
| hybrid meter | a time signature that combines simple time and compound time (for example, $\frac{5}{4}$ or $\frac{7}{8}$) |
| imitation | the repetition of a motive, complete music idea, or phrase, in another voice or clef |
| imperfect cadence | a cadence that ends on the dominant (V) chord |
| interval | the distance between two notes |
| inversion | a compositional device in which the intervals of a melody are inverted |
| inverted | turned upside down |
| key | the specific scale on which a piece of music is based |
| key signature | a collection of sharps or flats at the beginning of the staff that indicates the key of the music |
| ledger lines | the short lines used for notes that are above or below the staff |
| major interval (maj) | the interval of a 2nd, 3rd, 6th, or 7th, as formed above the tonic of a major scale |
| major scale | a series of seven notes with the following pattern of tones and semitones: tone–tone–semitone–tone–tone–tone–semitone |
| major triad | a three-note chord that consists of a major 3rd and a perfect 5th above the root |
| measure | a group of beats or pulses between two bar lines |
| melodic interval | the distance between two notes played one after the other |

| | |
|---|---|
| melodic minor scale | a scale formed by raising the sixth and seventh degrees of the natural minor scale ascending, and lowering the sixth and seventh degrees descending (There are semitones between notes $\hat{2}$ and $\hat{3}$ and notes $\hat{7}$ and $\hat{8}(\hat{1})$ ascending, and between notes $\hat{6}$ and $\hat{5}$ and notes $\hat{3}$ and $\hat{2}$ descending.) |
| minor interval (min) | the interval of a 2nd, 3rd, 6th, or 7th that is one semitone smaller than the equivalent major interval |
| minor scale | see **natural minor scale**, **harmonic minor scale**, and **melodic minor scale** |
| minor triad | a three-note chord that consists of a minor 3rd and a perfect 5th above the root |
| modern vocal score | an open score for four voices (soprano, alto, tenor, and bass) using three treble clefs and a bass clef (The clef for the tenor voice has an "8" underneath indicating that the notes sound an octave lower than written.) |
| motive | a short, melodic or rhythmic idea upon which a musical piece is based |
| natural | the sign that cancels a sharp or a flat |
| natural minor scale | a minor scale written with no changes from the key signature (There are semitones between notes $\hat{2}$ and $\hat{3}$ and notes $\hat{5}$ and $\hat{6}$.) |
| note | a written symbol used to indicate sound in music |
| open position | a chord position in which the notes are spread over an octave or more |
| open score | a score with a separate staff for each voice or instrument |
| octatonic scale | an eight note scale consisting of a strict alternation of tones and semitones |
| pentatonic scale | a five-note scale (one example is found on the black keys of the keyboard) |
| perfect cadence | a chord progression that consists of a dominant triad moving to a tonic triad (V–I) |
| perfect interval (per) | an interval of a unison, 4th, 5th, or 8ve as formed above the tonic of a major scale |
| plagal cadence | a chord progression that consists of a subdominant triad moving to a tonic triad (IV–I) |
| quadruplet | in compound time, a group of four notes that are played in the time of three notes of the same value |
| quintuplet | a group of five notes that are played in the time of three, four, or six notes of the same value, depending on the time signature |
| relative keys | major and minor keys that use the same key signature (The relative minor of a major key is three semitones lower: for example, the relative minor of D major is B minor.) |
| rest | a written symbol used to indicate silence in music |
| root | the fundamental note of a triad or chord |
| root position | the position of a chord when the root is the lowest note |
| scale | a series of notes with a specific pattern of tones and semitones |
| second inversion | the position of a chord when the fifth is the lowest note |
| semitone | one half step; the shortest distance between two notes on the keyboard |
| septuplet | a group of seven notes that are played in the time of four or six notes of the same value |
| sequence | the exact repetition of a passage at a lower or higher pitch |
| sextuplet | a group of six notes that are played in the time of four notes of the same value |

# GLOSSARY

| | |
|---|---|
| sharp ♯ | the sign that raises the pitch of a note one semitone |
| short score | a score for four voices (soprano, alto, tenor, and bass) written on two staves |
| simple duple time | time signatures that indicate two beats in each measure—for example, $\frac{2}{2}$, $\frac{2}{4}$, $\frac{2}{8}$ —where each beat is divisible by two |
| simple quadruple time | time signatures that indicate four beats in each measure—for example, $\frac{4}{2}$, $\frac{4}{4}$, $\frac{4}{8}$ —where each beat is divisible by two |
| simple time | time signatures in which each beat is divisible by two |
| simple triple time | time signatures that indicate three beats in each measure—for example, $\frac{3}{2}$, $\frac{3}{4}$, $\frac{3}{8}$ —where each beat is divisible by two |
| staff (*pl.* staves) | the five horizontal lines on and between which notes are written |
| string quartet score | an open instrumental score for first and second violins, viola, and cello that has four staves (written with two treble clefs, an alto clef, and a bass clef) |
| syncopation | a shift of accent from a strong beat to a weak beat |
| tenor clef | a clef that indicates the location of middle C on the fourth line of the staff |
| third | in a chord, the note that is a 3rd above the root |
| time signature | two numbers placed at the beginning of a piece of music (The upper number indicates the number of beats in each measure; the lower number indicates which note gets the beat.) |
| tonic | the first note of a scale |
| tonic major | a major scale that has the same tonic as a given minor scale (For example, the tonic major of D minor is D major.) |
| tonic minor | a minor scale that has the same tonic as a given minor scale (For example, the tonic minor of G major is G minor.) |
| transposition | the rewriting of a melody at a different pitch or in a different key |
| treble clef, G clef 𝄞 | the clef that indicates the location of G on the second line of the staff |
| triplet | a group of three notes played in the time of two notes of the same value |
| tritone | the interval of a diminished 5th or its enharmonic equivalent, an augmented 4th |
| whole tone | two semitones; the distance between any two keys with one key (white or black) between them |